T0252529

CYBERCULTURE THEORISTS

This book surveys a 'cluster' of works that seek to explore the cultures of cyberspace, the Internet and the information society. It introduces key ideas, and includes detailed discussion of the work of two key thinkers in this area, Manuel Castells and Donna Haraway, as well as outlining the development of cyberculture studies as a field. To do this, the book also explores selected 'moments' in this development, from the early 1990s, when cyberspace and cyberculture were only just beginning to come together as ideas, up to the present day, when the field of cyberculture studies has grown and bloomed, producing innovative theoretical and empirical work from a diversity of standpoints. Key topics include:

* life on the screen
* network society
* space of flows
* cyborg methods

Cyberculture Theorists is the ideal starting point for anyone wanting to understand how to theorize cyberculture in all its myriad forms.

David Bell is Senior Lecturer in Critical Human Geography at the University of Leeds. Recent publications include *The Cybercultures Reader* (2000), *An Introduction to Cybercultures* (2001) and *Cyberculture: The Key Concepts* (2004).

ROUTLEDGE CRITICAL THINKERS
essential guides for literary studies

Series Editor: Robert Eaglestone, Royal Holloway, University of London

Routledge Critical Thinkers is a series of accessible introductions to key figures in contemporary critical thought.

With a unique focus on historical and intellectual contexts, the volumes in this series examine important theorists':

- significance
- motivation
- key ideas and their sources
- impact on other thinkers

Concluding with extensively annotated guides to further reading, *Routledge Critical Thinkers* are the student's passport to today's most exciting critical thought.

Already available:

Louis Althusser by Luke Ferretter
Roland Barthes by Graham Allen
Jean Baudrillard by Richard J. Lane
Simone de Beauvoir by Ursula Tidd
Homi K. Bhabha by David Huddart
Maurice Blanchot by Ullrich Haase and William Large
Judith Butler by Sara Salih
Gilles Deleuze by Claire Colebrook
Jacques Derrida by Nicholas Royle
Michel Foucault by Sara Mills
Sigmund Freud by Pamela Thurschwell
Stuart Hall by James Procter
Martin Heidegger by Timothy Clark
Fredric Jameson by Adam Roberts

For further details on this series, see www.routledge.com/literature/series.asp

CYBERCULTURE THEORISTS

Manuel Castells and Donna Haraway

David Bell

Routledge
Taylor & Francis Group

LONDON AND NEW YORK

First published 2007
by Routledge
2 Park Square, Milton Park, Abingdon, Oxon, OX14 4RN

Simultaneously published in the USA and Canada
by Routledge
270 Madison Ave, New York, NY 10016

Routledge is an imprint of the Taylor & Francis Group, an informa business

Transferred to Digital Printing 2007

© 2007 David Bell

Typeset in Perpetua, Arial and Helvetica by
Taylor & Francis Books

All rights reserved. No part of this book may be reprinted or reproduced or utilized in any form
or by any electronic, mechanical, or other means, now known or hereafter invented, including
photocopying and recording, or in any information storage or retrieval system, without
permission in writing from the publishers.

Every effort has been made to ensure that the advice and information in this book is true and
accurate at the time of going to press. However, neither the publisher nor the authors can
accept any legal responsibility or liability for any errors or omissions that may be made. In the
case of drug administration, any medical procedure or the use of technical equipment
mentioned within this book, you are strongly advised to consult the manufacturer's guidelines.

British Library Cataloguing in Publication Data
A catalogue record for this book is available from the British Library

Library of Congress Cataloging in Publication Data
Bell, David, 1965 Feb. 12-
   Cyberculture theorists : Manuel Castells and Donna Haraway / by David Bell.
      p. cm. – (Routledge critical thinkers)
   Includes bibliographical references and index.
1. Cyberspace–Social aspects. 2. Information technology–Social aspects. 3. Castells,
Manuel. 4. Haraway, Donna Jeanne. I. Title. II. Series.
   HM851.B44 2006
   303.48'34–dc22   2006006203

ISBN10: 0-415-32430-0 ISBN13: 978-0-415-32430-4 (hbk)
ISBN10: 0-415-32431-9 ISBN13: 978-0-415-32431-1 (pbk)
ISBN10: 0-203-35701-9 ISBN13: 978-0-203-35701-9 (ebk)

Printed and bound by CPI Antony Rowe, Eastbourne

CONTENTS

SERIES EDITOR'S PREFACE

The books in this series offer introductions to major critical thinkers who have influenced literary studies and the humanities. The *Routledge Critical Thinkers* series provides the books you can turn to first when a new name or concept appears in your studies.

Each book will equip you to approach these thinkers' original texts by explaining their key ideas, putting them into context and, perhaps most importantly, showing you why they are considered to be significant. The emphasis is on concise, clearly written guides which do not presuppose a specialist knowledge. Although the focus is on particular figures, the series stresses that no critical thinker ever existed in a vacuum but, instead, emerged from a broader intellectual, cultural and social history. Finally, these books will act as a bridge between you and their original texts: not replacing them but rather complementing what they wrote. In some cases, volumes consider small clusters of thinkers working in the same area, developing similar ideas or influencing each other.

These books are necessary for a number of reasons. In his 1997 autobiography, *Not Entitled*, the literary critic Frank Kermode wrote of a time in the 1960s:

> On beautiful summer lawns, young people lay together all night, recovering from their daytime exertions and listening to a troupe of Balinese musicians. Under

their blankets or their sleeping bags, they would chat drowsily about the gurus
of the time … What they repeated was largely hearsay; hence my lunchtime
suggestion, quite impromptu, for a series of short, very cheap books offering
authoritative but intelligible introductions to such figures.

There is still a need for 'authoritative and intelligible introductions'. But
this series reflects a different world from the 1960s. New thinkers have
emerged and the reputations of others have risen and fallen, as new
research has developed. New methodologies and challenging ideas have
spread through the arts and humanities. The study of literature is no
longer – if it ever was – simply the study and evaluation of poems, novels
and plays. It is also the study of the ideas, issues and difficulties which
arise in any literary text and in its interpretation. Other arts and humanities subjects have changed in analogous ways.

With these changes, new problems have emerged. The ideas and issues
behind these radical changes in the humanities are often presented
without reference to wider contexts or as theories which you can simply
'add on' to the texts you read. Certainly, there's nothing wrong with
picking out selected ideas or using what comes to hand – indeed, some
thinkers have argued that this is, in fact, all we can do. However, it is
sometimes forgotten that each new idea comes from the pattern and
development of somebody's thought and it is important to study the
range and context of their ideas. Against theories 'floating in space', the
Routledge Critical Thinkers series places key thinkers and their ideas firmly
back in their contexts.

More than this, these books reflect the need to go back to the
thinkers' own texts and ideas. Every interpretation of an idea, even the
most seemingly innocent one, offers its own 'spin', implicitly or explicitly. To read only books on a thinker, rather than texts by that thinker, is to
deny yourself a chance of making up your own mind. Sometimes what
makes a significant figure's work hard to approach is not so much its style
or content as the feeling of not knowing where to start. The purpose of
these books is to give you a 'way in' by offering an accessible overview of
these thinkers' ideas and works and by guiding your further reading,
starting with each thinker's own texts. To use a metaphor from the
philosopher Ludwig Wittgenstein (1889 – 1951), these books are lad-
ders, to be thrown away after you have climbed to the next level. Not

only, then, do they equip you to approach new ideas, but also they empower you, by leading you back to a theorist's own texts and encouraging you to develop your own informed opinions.

Finally, these books are necessary because, just as intellectual needs have changed, the education systems around the world – the contexts in which introductory books are usually read – have changed radically, too. What was suitable for the minority higher education system of the 1960s is not suitable for the larger, wider, more diverse, high-technology education systems of the twenty-first century. These changes call not just for new, up-to-date introductions but new methods of presentation. The presentational aspects of *Routledge Critical Thinkers* have been developed with today's students in mind.

Each book in the series has a similar structure. They begin with a section offering an overview of the life and ideas of the featured thinkers and explaining why they are important. The central section of each book discusses the thinkers' key ideas, their context, evolution and reception: a book that deasl with more than one thinker also explains and explores the influence of each on each. The volumes conclude with a survey of the impact of the thinker or thinkers, outlining how their ideas have been taken up and developed by others. In addition, there is a detailed final section suggesting and describing books for further reading. This is not a 'tacked-on' section but an integral part of each volume. In the first part of this section you will find brief descriptions of the key works by the featured thinkers, then, following this, information on the most useful critical works and, in some cases, on relevant websites. This section will guide you in your reading, enabling you to follow your interests and develop your own projects. Throughout each book, references are given in what is known as the Harvard system (the author and the date of a work cited are given in the text and you can look up the full details in the list of further reading at the back). This offers a lot of information in very little space. The books also explain technical terms and use boxes to describe events or ideas in more detail, away from the main emphasis of the discussion. Boxes are also used at times to highlight definitions of terms frequently used or coined by a thinker. In this way, the boxes serve as a kind of glossary, easily identified when flicking through the book.

The thinkers in the series are 'critical' for three reasons. First, they are examined in the light of subjects which involve criticism: principally literary studies or English and cultural studies, but also other disciplines which rely on the criticism of books, ideas, theories and unquestioned assumptions. Second, they are critical because studying their work will provide you with a 'toolkit' for your own informed critical reading and thought, which will make you critical. Third, these thinkers are critical because they are crucially important: they deal with ideas and questions which can overturn conventional understandings of the world, of texts, of everything we take for granted, leaving us with a deeper understanding of what we already knew and with new ideas.

No introduction can tell you everything. However, by offering a way into critical thinking, this series hopes to begin to engage you in an activity which is productive, constructive and potentially life-changing.

ACKNOWLEDGEMENTS

Thanks to Bob Eaglestone, Series Editor, and to Katrina Chandler at Routledge, for their encouragement and patience. Thanks to colleagues and students, past and present, especially at Staffordshire University and Manchester Metropolitan University. Special thanks to Joanne for cheering my email updates on the book's progress, and to Daisy, Ruth and Jon, as ever.

WHY CYBERCULTURE?

This is a book about cyberculture theorists; its aim is to introduce a small handful of key thinkers and their ideas, with two discussed in more detail, to provide a kind of overview of cyberculture theory. This has been a phenomenal growth area in terms of academic work, as scholars across a range of different disciplines from computing to philosophy, cultural studies to geography, have sought to understand and explain the world we now live in. Now, we have to call this enterprise something. There has been a huge debate about names in relation to this topic, big arguments about the best and worst words to use. I have chosen to stick with certain words, words like cyberspace and cyberculture, and I hope to be able to explain why here. Let's ask some more questions ...

WHY CYBERSPACE?

How are we going to talk about the world we now live in? Who is 'we' (or, as Sherry Turkle (1996) cutely asks, 'Who am we?'), what counts as living, where is this world? Although many would disagree with me, I still like to talk about cyberspace. I think there is something expansive about this term, this metaphor for an imaginary space that exists in, on and between 'computational devices' (another of Turkle's useful terms). I like to corral all kinds of things together in cyberspace; not just computers and software, but also digital devices such as MP3 players, or BlackBerrys, or new medical imaging technologies, cyberpets, digital animations and simulations of all kinds – and so the list goes on. All these things, and many more besides, are connected together, in some way or another. They are part of the same kin group, to borrow from Donna Haraway (2004a). But cyberspace also exists in the imagination, in fiction, in the stories we tell ourselves about this world (Bell 2001).

I also like the term because it has a quaint tinge of nostalgia to it; or, rather, what we might call technostalgia. It's oddly old-fashioned, antique even, yet there's something wrapped inside it as a word, something belying its roots in science fiction, something even maybe a little bit utopian. Cyberspace: it sounds like the future was supposed to be. So, while countless minds have been stretched by the task of defining cyberspace – and then stretched some more by arguing about competing definitions and about the usefulness of the term – I hope you will indulge me in the practice of its continued use. But what happens when the word is disassembled, back to its cyber- prefix (borrowed from cybernetics) and -space suffix, and then recombined with another dread word for many thinkers, 'culture'? We shall see in a while.

So cyberspace, as the legend goes, is a word birthed in what cyber-punk writer William Gibson called a 'neologic spasm'. Gibson is famously credited with prefiguring cyberspace in his cyberpunk novel *Neuromancer* (1984), coining the term to describe the imaginary 'datascape' which his characters entered by 'jacking in' – connecting their consciousness directly to networked computers. The well-known and often-quoted for-mulation in *Neuromancer* runs like this:

> *Cyberspace.* A consensual hallucination experienced daily by millions of legiti-mate operators. ... A graphic representation of data abstracted from the banks of every computer in the human system. Unthinkable complexity. Lines of light ranged in the nonspace of the mind, clusters and constellations of data. Like city lights, receding.
>
> (Gibson 1984: 67)

This vivid description offered a powerful fictional portent for the future, a future of unthinkable complexity and constellations of data. However,

CYBERNETICS

A theory of the control and communication of regulatory feedback in biological, sociotechnical or social systems. Changes to the external environment are looped back to the system, which makes adjustments to maintain a steady state. The term 'cybernetics' stems from the Greek word *kubernites*, meaning steersman, governor, pilot or rudder. Cybernetics is the science of communication and control in living beings or machines. The modern study of cybernetics began around the time of the Second World War, bringing together developments in a number of disciplines. The name 'cybernetics' was coined by scientist Norbert Wiener to denote the study of 'teleological mechanisms' and was popularized through his book *Cybernetics, or Control and Communication in the Animal and Machine* (1948). Wiener popularized the social implications of cybernetics, drawing analogies between automatic systems such as a regulated steam engine and human institutions in his best-selling *The Human Use of Human Beings: Cybernetics and Society* (1950).

the computing science realities of what was then emerging as cyberspace were little-known to Gibson; nevertheless, the term and the way cyberspace was depicted in *Neuromancer* have had a profound influence upon its development and its representation – an influence even Gibson admits he didn't foresee when he cobbled the word together. He writes in the short essay 'Academy Leader' (1991) about the setting loose of such neologisms, about how terms and concepts take on their own life, and spread and mutate, like a virus or a 'meme' (a kind of thought or idea virus that spreads through culture):

> Assembled word *cyberspace* from small and readily available components of language. Neologic spasm: the primal act of pop poetics. Preceded any concept whatever. Slick and hollow – awaiting received meaning. All I did: folded words as taught. Now other words accrete in the interstices.
>
> (Gibson 1991: 27)

This conceptualization, fleshed out into what some commentators named 'Gibsonian cyberspace', was not only mapped out in cyberpunk, of course. Computer scientists, theorists of all sorts, hackers and others, were among those attempting to conjure the space between the screens: to bring forth a new realm, a virtual realm, a consensual hallucination. So while some have argued that the term is too vague or dated now, preferring to talk of digital this or new media that, I maintain that cyberspace nevertheless has some enduring appeal and conceptual purchase, folding together technologies, uses and users, experiences, stories and images. For that reason, cyberspace is still a useful metonym.

CYBERCULTURE

Of course, cyberspace is seen as the host or hive of much memetic and viral diffusion and infection, too (Thieme 2000). Now, while *Neuromancer* is conventionally fingered as the origin-text for cyberspace, as the source code for later developers of the hard- and software (Stone 1995), the birthplace and birthdate of the term 'cyberculture' is more obscure and uncertain. It was being used quite widely in academia by the mid-1990s, certainly, and was defined earlier than that by American critic Mark Dery as:

> A far-flung, loosely knit complex of sublegitimate, alternative, and oppositional sub-cultures whose common project is the subversive use of technocommodities often framed by radical body politics ... Cyberculture is divisible into several major territories: visionary technology, fringe science, avant-garde art, and pop culture.
>
> (Dery 1992: 509)

CYBERPUNK

This is a subgenre of science fiction literature and film, with its origins in the 1980s, and associated with writers such as William Gibson, Bruce Sterling and Neal Stephenson (though it is arguably prefigured in work by, among others, Philip K. Dick, William Burroughs, J. G. Ballard). In cinema, films like *Blade Runner* (1982) are seen as encapsulating the spirit and aesthetic of cyberpunk. Cyberpunk centres on the impacts of new technologies such as computers and virtual reality, and with propagating popular images of cyberspace, cyborgs, artificial life forms and so on. Like many literary and filmic genres, it has split and recombined, with sub-sub-genres including steam punk, biopunk and cyberprep, the latter offering a slick, clean, rosy view of the future to contrast cyberpunk's dirty, grim dystopias.

This, however, is a somewhat narrower definition than I shall be utilizing here, and what Dery describes above I have previously labelled 'cybersubcultures' (Bell 2001). My more expansive definition of cyberculture, the one that informs the shape and scope of this book, uses the term to denote a number of things simultaneously, as reflected in the breadth and diversity of topics and emphases stretched across the subject. For me, cyberculture is a way of thinking about how people and digital technologies interact, how we *live together* – so the suffix 'culture' is used in that elastic way that one of the founding fathers of British cultural studies, Raymond Williams (1976), uses it, to talk of *ways of life*. This view of the 'culture' in cultural studies is also drawn on by Frow and Morris (2000: 316), who define culture neatly as 'a network of embedded practices and representations (texts, images, talk, codes of behavior, and the narrative structures organizing these) that shapes every aspect of social life'. Cyberculture therefore refers here to ways of life in cyberspace, or ways of life shaped by cyberspace, where cyberspace is a matrix of embedded practices and representations. While cyberculture is certainly a 'contested and evolving discourse' (Bell et al. 2004: xiii), one that is hard to keep up with, if we keep in mind the most expansive definition, as offered here, then I think we will get along just fine.

As I have also argued before, we need to look at the stories that are told about these ways of life; stories that have material, symbolic and experiential variants (Bell 2001). Telling material stories about cyberculture includes tales about the hardware and software, the prehistories and histories of the material cultures of new information and communications technologies. But material storytelling also needs to attend to the materialized relations between people and these technologies, for to understand material culture must mean to also understand uses, interactions, the thoughts and feelings that our relationships evoke (Dant 2005). And this also means looking at the crucial issues of distribution, access and inequality, for the possibility of building relationships with what Turkle (1995) called these 'intimate machines' is structured at different scales, from the global to the local, by persistent patterns of inequality, creating the so-called digital divide, a new class system (yet one that also reproduces much older iniquities) based on access to information. What we might call the political economy of cyberculture is therefore a vital piece of the bigger story, especially when we rub it up against the more utopian discourses of the digital global village or virtual community (Bell 2001).

Such utopianism, which is in itself multi-stranded, is an important thread of the various symbolic tales that have a key role to play in storying cyberculture. Thinking about cyberculture involves thinking about representations, meanings, images: about the ways in which we assemble particular narratives about how these new technologies have changed, are changing, or will change our lives. It also means constructing that 'we' whose lives have changed, are changing, or will change, and this often means invisibilizing those people on the 'wrong side' of the digital divide. These symbolic stories 'package' cyberculture for us, providing a frame of meaning, and clusters of connotation. There are, of course, radically different repertoires and registers in this almanac of stories: there are those provided by journalism, by advertising, by fiction, by academia, by politics. There are mundane stories and there are spectacular stories. These can be positive, even utopian, but they can also be negative and dystopian. Such stories are in endless circulation and reiteration, and they help give shape to the stories we in turn tell ourselves about our own place in cyberculture.

Hence the third strand, experiential stories. My argument is that we experience our interactions with new technologies as a folding-together of material and symbolic tales. Sitting at a computer, logged onto the Internet, for example, we are constantly clicking between the embodied sensations of staring at a screen and typing and the disembodied dream of surfing cyberspace as uploaded consciousness, but also connecting to other stories, other images and ideas – for example, ideas about the 'world wide web' as a free source of information on an infinite multitude of topics, or ideas about the new forms of connectivity between people that the Internet has provided. Maybe we remember a scene from, say, *The Matrix*, and feel for a moment like Neo. Or maybe the 'ambient fear' of computer viruses pervades our time online, making us anxious, suspicious of any spam emails we receive, guarded about where we go searching, spooked by pop-ups or attachments, wary of infection. Our minds are full of such hyperlinks, such intertextuality, and our everyday interactions with new technologies are patterned by this continual flickering. Paul Taylor (2001) refers to this experience as 'living in the gap' between symbolic imaginings of cyberspace and the 'realities' of life with these technologies. We are infected, he writes, with 'futuristic flu' – run down and tired out by the connectivity and interactiveness, yet still seduced by its promises. A lot of the experiential stories we shall encounter in this book are mundane, ordinary stories of people like you and me struggling to make sense with our connections and disconnections to cyberculture. This is in itself symptomatic of the cultural studies approach:

> Cultural studies often tends to operate in what looks like an eccentric way, starting with the particular, the detail, the scrap of ordinary or banal existence, and then working to unpack the density of relations and of intersecting social domains that inform it.
>
> (Frow and Morris 2000: 327)

Such eccentricity, I hope to show, provides a particularly fruitful way into understand the 'contested and evolving discourse' and practices of cyberculture.

So, we have now spent some time thinking about the suffix 'culture', and about cultural studies – but what of its prefix, 'cyber'? This has its own origin stories, too, such as its connection to cybernetics and therefore to particular understandings of the relationships between bodies, minds and machines. Some critics have argued that this prefix is now obsolete, like some old software that's been superceded by version 2.0. Hence the use instead of words like 'new', or 'digital'. Some writers seem uncertain what to call this thing of ours any more (see Silver 2004): digital culture, new media, ICTs (though I am well aware each of these has its own specific meaning, they do also nest together).

One reason for this bewilderment is the diversifying (and also converging) of technologies and uses. We are blurring boundaries between different kinds of technologies, different functions and uses, different stories (Marshall 2004). It's hard to keep up. This frenetic churning of new technologies, uses and meanings is, of course, another dominant strand in the stories I have sketched: the idea that newness is necessary and valuable, that keeping up is important (and being left behind is to be feared). Things get faster, smaller, more useful, more user-friendly, and this is a good thing – or so one particular type of storytelling says. Other stories, less often told, reveal the trials, the resistances, the accommodations and negotiations involved in living with new (or however we want to name them) technologies (see Lehtonen 2003).

Now, one consequence of the circulation of this kind of story is that it places people in a *passive* position: technology is 'done' to us. This kind of formulation, sometimes referred to as technological determinism, has been subject to sustained critique from scholars arguing that things aren't so simple, that this relationship is more interactive, many-layered and complex: technology is socially shaped in all kinds of ways. There are good stories here, too, of the happenstance development of technologies and uses, from email and texting (SMS) to webcams. But at the symbolic (and therefore also at the experiential) level, lots of people *do* feel that they are in a deterministic relationship with these new technologies, that they are relatively powerless, that the makers and sellers of these things are in control, and that sometimes the technology itself is in control, too. So I think it is important to register determinism, to acknowledge its potency as a commonsense way in which lots of us experience and articulate our relationships with the intimate machines we live with (as well as those we don't live with, or won't live with). But it is equally important to run it alongside other ways of thinking, other stories. That has been one of my ambitions here: to highlight some theorists and theories so as to put divergent viewpoints, different stories, in close proximity.

Cyberculture, however contested the term may now be, also designates a field of academic inquiry, also contested. Necessary post- or

TECHNOLOGICAL DETERMINISM

The idea that technology affects society in a one-way relationship: technology is something done to society, to people, who passively experience its effects. This brackets technology off from society, however, rather than seeing the two complexly co-related – technology arises in a social context, and is shaped by use. Theorists thus talk of the **social construction of technology** perspective (see p. 39) as a corrective to technological determinism. However, we must recognize the popular circulation of deterministic thinking, as it affects how people respond to technology in their everyday lives.

trans-disciplinary, 'cyberculture studies' represents the coming together of diverse strands of academic work across a range of subject areas. As such, it is work carried out in a diversity of intellectual and institutional locations, often embedded within more 'traditional' subjects and departments; Michael Benedikt (1991c: 23) wrote at the dawning of the cyberculture age that 'every discipline can have an interest in the enterprise of creating [and theorizing] cyberspace, a contribution to make, and a historical narrative to justify both'. This openness gives cyberculture studies a heterodox richness, and an anti-canonical stance: it is both theoretically and methodologically promiscuous – as Frow and Morris (2000: 327, 332) say of cultural studies more broadly, there is a commitment to 'methodological impurity' and 'rigorous mixing'. But this can also make it seem like a fringe activity, not a 'proper' subject. Its 'newbie' status makes it seem faddish, and its promiscuity can be taken as heretical. To my mind these are advantages, signalling an openness that many 'traditional' subjects lack. So, to sketch its parameters rather than attempting a strict definition, let's say that cyberculture studies includes (*among others, and in no particular order*):

- work in computer science and other related 'cybertechnosciences', including hardware and software development and user modelling, robotics, artificial intelligence (AI) and artificial life (A-Life), nano-technoscience and so on;
- insights from the history of science and technology, for example on the histories of computing;
- sociological studies of the uses, users and impacts of and on new technologies;
- ideas from science and technology studies about how to understand 'actor-networks' of people and technologies;
- work by geographers on the spaces of cyberspace, and work in urban studies on 'cybercities';
- literary theories and studies, for example those concerned with science fiction and cyberpunk;
- media studies work on new media, multimedia or digital media, and film studies work on sci-fi cinema, digital film-making, new modes of film production, distribution and consumption;

- philosophy of science and technology, and philosophical theories used to think about cyberspace and cyberculture;
- economics and organization studies of changing work patterns in the information and knowledge economies;
- feminist studies of science and technology, including 'cyberfeminisms' and 'cyborg feminisms';
- social, political and cultural theory in its diverse forms;
- research in the biomedical and biotech sciences on the interfaces between bodies and technologies, such as gene therapies or xenotransplantation;
- policy-oriented studies, whether in social, welfare, communications, cultural or new, hybrid 'cyberpolicy' contexts;
- studies of the creative and applied arts intersecting with new technologies, and studies of the aesthetics of new technologies;
- work on 'cyberpsychology' – the psychological impacts of cyberspace;
- research in linguistics into the languages of new technologies and their users;
- cross-disciplinary futurology that predicts ways of living yet to come;
- cultural studies approaches to understanding the material, symbolic and experiential dimensions of cyberspace, to cybercultural forms, practices, politics and identities, and to cybercultural production and consumption.

As such, cyberculture studies is a complex field (or post-field) which not only makes use of diverse academic traditions and theoretical perspectives, but also deploys a diversity of research methods and approaches.

In a useful overview, David Silver (2000) identifies three co-evolutionary strands to cyberculture studies. The first he labels 'popular cyberculture'. This strand includes journalistic accounts of experiences online, branched into utopian and dystopian forms. The former is best exemplified by the establishment of new magazines discussing cyberspace, such as *Wired* and *Mondo 2000* (on the latter, see Sobchack 2000), while the latter often took the form of populist books offering portents of doom about the digital age – for example, Mark Slouka's (1995) critique of the virtual, *War of the Worlds*, and Clifford Stoll's (1995) sceptical *Silicon Snake Oil*.

This first bloom of publishing overlaps in Silver's account with a second phase, 'cyberculture studies', in which journalistic or popular accounts rub shoulders with work engaging with bodies of theory, and with key interests in online identity, community and communication – mapping the *social effects* of cyberspace (this is discussed here via the work of Sherry Turkle). The third stage, 'critical cyberculture studies', is marked by the more systematic development and deployment of 'theory', and by a broadening out of focus as more and more academics and commentators set their sights on cyberspace.

Silver's typology is a useful sketch, and it is important to highlight key turning points in the development of the field, often signalled by landmark publications. These include Michael Benedikt's (1991a) *Cyberspace: First Steps*, which defined a set of perspectives combining philosophy with social, cultural and literary theory, to explore the evolving 'shape' of cyberspace; Benedikt's own essays from this landmark collection are discussed later. Another obvious landmark is Donna Haraway's (1991) 'Cyborg Manifesto' – given extended treatment in this book, and an essay that defined feminist engagements with cyberspace and the subdiscipline of 'cyborg studies' or 'cyborgology'. Equally important defining texts from the same era include Mark Dery's (1994) *FlameWars* and Larry McCaffery's (1991) *Storming the Reality Studio*, both of which mix academic and creative writing, with a heavy emphasis on cyberpunk.

By the mid-1990s, cyberculture studies was witnessing something of a publishing boom, representing both a consolidation and a diversification. By this time it is possible to discern significant threads within cyberculture studies, in part reflecting vestigial disciplinary imperatives – for example, the emphasis on empirically-grounded studies from a more sociological tradition, as against textual and / or representational analyses from a cultural or literary studies perspective. In this book I focus more on the former, exemplified below by the work of Maria Bakardjieva and Manuel Castells. In addition, cyberculture studies has birthed its own 'schools', such as feminist cyberstudies and cyborg studies, and has developed a series of key concerns, including issues of the body / mind split, questions of posthumanism or postbiology (artificial life, artificial intelligence), and a focus on key social issues such as identity and community (see Bell 2001). The consolidation of cyberculture studies is also marked by a blossoming in the publication of textbooks, dictionaries, readers and specialized journals, as well as by an expansive presence on university curricula and, of course, in cyberspace itself. While not yet displaying the patina of more traditional disciplines, cyberculture studies has certainly taken root, and also born strange fruit.

At the same time, developments in new technologies and their uses and meanings have kept cyberculture very visible outside the academy, reflecting its increasing embeddedness in everyday life. From the Millennium Bug to the dot.com crash, popular stories about the promises and perils of cyberculture also proliferate. So, in the first decade of this new millennium, cyberculture studies continues to develop, and to move in innovative directions. It retains an openness to different approaches and perspectives, reflected in the continuing growth of interest in understanding what happens when people and technologies come together in increasingly complex comminglings.

Silver's typology provides a useful brief history of cyberculture studies, while a more programmatic attempt to define 'cultural studies of the Internet' can be found in Jonathan Sterne's 'Thinking the Internet: Cultural Studies Versus the Millennium' (1999). This is an important article in that it attempts to lay out a specifically cultural studies approach to cyberspace, therefore productively exemplifying Silver's critical cyberculture phase. Sterne provides a road map of what cultural studies as a discipline uniquely brings to analysis of cyberspace, urging scholars to 'move beyond the commonplaces and clichés of Internet scholarship and [to] reconceptualize it in intellectually challenging and politically vital terms' (Sterne 1999: 260). It is, perhaps, in the last part of that statement – about being politically vital – that Sterne's essay is most insightful; he reminds scholars of the deep political commitment at the heart of the cultural studies project, arguing that if it is (or should be) about anything, then cultural studies is about culture and power. Any critical study of the Internet should therefore have at its heart an analysis of culture and power, hence my focus on cyberculture theory.

To advance his argument, Sterne places emphasis on the need to understand and analyse critically the politics of knowledge production (asking what is at stake in studying the Internet, and how new knowledge of cyberspace can advance emancipatory politics), the need to be acutely aware of context (the manifold relationships between people, place, practices and things) and the need to produce a theory of articulation (how things are connected together). Such a theory would have as its central concerns '(a) *what counts* in a cultural study of the Internet and (b) *how to think about* and represent the Internet' (Sterne 1999: 263; emphasis in original). Finally, and echoing points made earlier, Sterne reinforces the necessity of a commitment to theory as a way of finding new and more effective ways to describe and analyse cyberspace and cyberculture.

Making a point resonant with Silver's discussion of critical cyberculture studies, Sterne calls for a move beyond the simplistic online / offline (or virtual / real) split which has for so long impaired analyses of cyberspace, towards a conceptualization that emphasizes understanding the place of the Internet in everyday life, a point made clearly in the work of Bakardjieva discussed shortly. Equally importantly, Sterne argues for the need to reconnect the Internet to other media, and to techniques of analysing other media. This is particularly crucial in the current period, given the increasing convergence of new (and old) media. As new digital devices such as MP3 players and palm pilots become more and more ubiquitous, and as existing media are repurposed for the digital age (mobile phones, for example), so the idea of separating out the Internet as an object of study becomes redundant (Marshall 2004). At the same time, the uses to which we may now put our computers – from listening to the radio to editing home movies to shopping – call for a broader rethinking of what it is we are studying when we're studying cyberculture.

This last point is worth exploring in a bit more detail. Some researchers have suggested that we need to track the myriad sites where we encounter digital culture beyond the narrow emphasis on the computer screen: cyberspace exists in all kinds of places, from CGI-heavy movies to imaging technologies used in biomedicine (see Bell 2001). Moreover, the kinds of contact we have with these new technologies are equally varied: we may be transformed into data and lodged in databases thanks to the manifold technologies of data collection that monitor our habits and routines (from our shopping practices to our workplace productivity); equally, we may have particularly intimate relationships with devices that become part of our everyday lives, even part of our bodies – leading some scholars to theorize the body–technology interface by using ideas of the cyborg or the posthuman. Cyberspace is a constantly changing landscape, and our theories must be equally adaptable: writing about cyberculture is intensely time-sensitive, as already noted.

My aim in producing this guide has been, therefore, to try to reflect, *but not to define*, this still-morphing field. Like the ever-changing technologies and uses, the ideas and stories about them are hard to keep up with; nevertheless, I have tried to knot together a set of threads that carries these heterogeneities and complexities – a cat's cradle of cybercultures (Haraway 2004b [1992]). The next chapter of the book discusses three 'moments' in cyberculture theory, in an effort to map some key changes in this disorderly field. The works discussed are two essays by Michael Benedikt from his landmark collection *Cyberspace: First Steps* (1991a), a book which came out just ahead of cyberspace; Sherry Turkle's (1995) *Life on the Screen*, included in Silver's (2000) discussion of second-wave 'cyberculture studies' and representative of the first flush of social and cultural commentary on cyberspace, and Maria Bakardjieva's (2005) *Internet Society*, which I think usefully exemplifies what Silver calls 'critical cyberculture studies' and which reflects some of the current directions cyberculture theory is heading. These works are selected to show different ways of thinking cyberculture, a trajectory then rounded out by a more detailed discussion of two key cybertheorists (though both would probably contest that label), Manuel Castells and Donna Haraway.

MOMENTS IN CYBERCULTURE

As a way into a tight focus on particular cyberculture theorists, I want to introduce here three writers – Michael Benedikt, Sherry Turkle and Maria Bakardjieva – whose work represents three phases of cyberculture research. These accounts give a flavour of the development of cyberculture theory, its methods and concerns, since the early 1990s. While the endless branching and bifurcating of cyberculture means I could have chosen countless alternatives, these three writers all do the useful job of summing up the mood of the time and place they were writing from.

1 CYBERSPACE: FIRST STEPS

Edited by Michael Benedikt, Hal Box Chair in Urbanism and Director of the Center for American Architecture and Design at the University of Texas at Austin, USA, *Cyberspace: First Steps* is based largely around papers presented at the self-proclaimed First Conference on Cyberspace, held at the same institution in May 1990. So the book does indeed contain a number of 'first steps', including landmark essays, still often cited, such as David Tomas's 'Old Rituals for New Space', Michael Heim's 'The Erotic Ontology of Cyberspace' and Alluquere Rosanne Stone's 'Will the Real Body Please Stand Up', as well as cyberpunk guru William Gibson's account of birthing the word cyberspace itself, 'Academy Leader'. It also includes two essays by the editor, which are the focus on my discussion here; given the heterogeneity of the chapters in the volume, it seems more fruitful to focus on these twins rather than to try to capture something of the buzz that still, more than a decade later, crackles through *Cyberspace: First Steps*.

Benedikt provides both a contextualizing and thematicizing introduction to the volume, and his own extensive essay which discusses how cyberspace might work. This future-facing orientation is important: the book was published ahead of cyberspace, signalling a beginning, an advent: 'Cyberspace itself is an elusive and future thing', Benedikt (1991c: 22) writes, adding that 'one can hardly be definitive at this early stage' about the forms it was then yet to take. This is one reason why I have chosen to discuss this work here; for its 'prefiguring' of cyberspace and cyberculture (see also Tofts, Jonson and Cavallaro 2002). There is a palpable sense of promise and excitement: 'the door to cyberspace is open' (ibid.: 18) and Benedikt is keen to step through. He also sees in the book, and in cyberspace, a 'motivating, unifying vision' of the future (Benedikt 1991b: 188) – a door to be leapt through enthusiastically, then.

His introduction to the book opens with ten vignettes, each one attempting to poetically capture what cyberspace was imagined as, at this time and place. I would love to quote them all, as they're all so evocative, but there isn't time for that here. Instead I give one full example from the ten, then select some choice cuts from the others:

> Cyberspace: The tablet become a page become a screen become a world, a virtual world. Everywhere and nowhere, a place where nothing is forgotten and yet everything changes.
>
> (Benedikt 1991c: 1)

Cyberspace is also summoned as a 'parallel universe', as a 'common mental geography', as forming 'wherever electricity runs with intelligence', as a 'realm of pure information, filling like a lake', as a 'soft hail of electrons', but also as 'an unhappy word' from the dystopian pen of William Gibson, here to be made happy again when removed from the cyberpunk domain and brought into computer science. (The 'category line' on the back of the book jacket, which signals the subject area of the

GIBSONIAN CYBERSPACE

Cyberpunk writer William Gibson famously coined the term 'cyberspace' to describe a 'virtual' landscape made up of all the information in the world, a description given fullest form in his novel *Neuromancer* (1984). Cyberspace is entered as disembodied consciousness, by 'jacking in' to the network, and the landscape is a battleground over the ownership of and access to data, between corporations and hackers. Gibsonian cyberspace thus refers to visions of cyberspace which trace back to Gibson's vivid descriptions. In some contexts, Gibsonian cyberspace is contrasted to Barlovian cyberspace, named after John Perry Barlow, the American cyber-guru, who is said to have first used 'cyberspace' to describe networked computing.

book to aid booksellers in shelving it appropriately, lists only Computer Science as the proper home of this book – cyberspace was not yet fully seen as of interest to those studying culture.)

That Gibson is here from the start is another key point: we are talking here about 'Gibsonian cyberspace' – the neologism coined to describe cyberspace as imagined in the shadow of its description in *Neuromancer* (1984). As Stone (1991) notes in this volume, *Neuromancer* had an incredible impact not just on sci-fi fans but also on computer scientists, hackers and academics. It became a kind of 'source code' for the development of cyberspace, and etched into the ideas presented in *Cyberspace: First Steps* is exactly that legacy, which informs, for example, Benedikt's own discussion of the 'datasphere' as an urban architectural form, as we shall see.

CYBERSPACE THREADS

Now, having laid out those ten conjurings of cyberspace, Benedikt hits the brake: 'Cyberspace as just described – and, for the most part, as described in this book – does not exist' (Benedikt 1991c: 3). *It does not exist* – yet. Or, rather, it exists in the minds of those imagining it, but does not yet exist as an everyday experience, as a 'thing'. It does not (yet) exist as the thing Benedikt later defines it as: 'a multisensory, three-dimensional, involving, richly textured and nuanced virtual world converting oceans of abstract data and the intelligence of distant people into perceptually engaging, all-but-firsthand experience' (Benedikt 1991b: 191). We might ask, here and now: does this cyberspace exist yet? Will it ever? Benedikt is himself sanguine about this issue in an interview from a decade later, as we shall see (Szeto 2002).

Using the Popperian idea of 'World 3' – the 'world' of patterns of communications that overlays Worlds 1 (the material world) and 2 (the subjective world of consciousness) – Benedikt uses his introduction to weave four intertwining historical threads that have evolved in World 3. One aim of this approach is to highlight the long history of cyberspace – that it has been coming for millennia. His first thread is perhaps best summarized by his term 'symbolic doing' (Benedikt 1991a.: 13) – representation, including pictures and writing, myths, stories. Human cultures need to live in stories, need rituals and magic, and cyberspace is coming to be 'the most tempting stage for the acting out of mythic realities', the prime site for symbolic storying (ibid.: 6; see also Bell 2001).

Benedikt's second thread is also about 'symbolic doing', this time encapsulated in the history of communications media, in its broadest sense, from writing to printing to transmission, storage and retrieval (hence his 'The tablet become a page become a screen ... ' formulation quoted above). Here he is concerned with the dematerialization of communication – or, perhaps, we might say its 'rematerialization' after it had first been materialized in printing, recording, photography, etc. Crucially, this dematerialization erases the constraints on communication made by geography, at all scales, from the global to the local (he gives the

WORLD 3

Austrian-born British philosopher Karl Popper (1902 – 98) proposed the idea of the existence of three 'worlds': World 1, the world of physical objects, events and biological entities; World 2, the world of mental events and objects; World 3, the world of products of the human mind, or abstract objects (theories, formulae, learning). He proposed that World 3 is partly autonomous from the other two, and that changes in World 3 can impact on Worlds 1 and 2. Today, World 3 is sometimes used to talk about cyberspace and cyberculture, as an emblematic abstract 'mind-space'.

excellent example of remote controls for TVs in the latter case). Moreover, the history lesson in thread two is also about widening access to media production as well as consumption – cameras, photocopiers, cassette recorders all put the tools for making content in ordinary people's hands. Cyberspace expands this potential exponentially.

The then-recent history of this thread is overshadowed, Benedikt (1991c: 11) writes, by the 'almost irrational enthusiasm' for virtual reality (VR). Indeed, VR overshadows much of *Cyberspace: First Steps*, as it did much of the writing and talking about cyberspace at that time. Benedikt notes how virtual reality was seen as superseding the 'symbolic doing' of threads one and two by reintroducing direct, 'post-symbolic' communication – a return of the literal – though he is unsure of how this will pan out: 'In future computer-mediated environments, whether or not this kind of literal, experiential sharing of worlds will supersede the symbolic, ideational, and implicit sharing of worlds embodied in the traditional mechanisms of text and representation remains to be seen' (ibid.: 13). With the benefit of hindsight, we can say that, at least where we've got to now, that idea is still a long, long way off, but also that people have found ingenious ways round the failure of VR to deliver such a cyberspace.

The third thread is, unsurprisingly given Benedikt's disciplinary background, about architecture. He argues that architecture is also part of World 3, the world of patterns of communication (just as 'natural architectures' such as ant colonies are) – architecture is communication in built form. Benedikt presents a take on the history of architecture in biblical terms, moreover; using ideas of nostalgia for Eden and of the

VIRTUAL REALITY (VR)

3-D, immersive, computer-generated audio-visual simulations of reality (or imaginings of reality), for a while widely seen as the most exciting new development in human – computer interactions. Applications such as flight simulation and battle training have been developed, but the technology has not evolved to match the hype that preceded it. VR has become more useful conceptually, in terms of troubling ideas about what is 'real', as well as being widely depicted in science fiction and cyberpunk.

Heavenly City from Revelation. Architecture is about transcendence, he writes, about a desire to go beyond – an idea which has led to the 'ephemeralization' or 'self-dematerialization' of architecture, as buildings become light, hollow, transparent. The Heavenly City epitomizes this impulse, this transcendent architecture: 'weightlessness, radiance, numerological complexity, palaces upon palaces, peace and harmony through rule by the good and wise, utter cleanliness, transcendence of nature and of crude beginnings, the availability of all things pleasurable and cultured' (ibid.: 15) – hardly Gibsonian cyberspace, then, given the latter's dystopian griminess (see Tomas 1991, 2000). Yet it is very like cyberspace, the city as information, the epitome of World 3 – a different way of imagining what Manuel Castells calls the space of flows (see later). Benedikt's bottom line is also unsurprising: building cyberspace will require cyberspace architects, designers of electronic edifices, the liquid architecture of information flows. In this respect, in the visual imaging of data arranged like skyscrapers or heavenly cities, he is, of course, purely Gibsonian.

The last of Benedikt's historical threads concerns the mathematics of space, both geometry and algebra. How is 'real' space theorized mathematically, and what does this mean for ways of thinking about cyberspace-as-space? Space is here seen more as a 'field of play' for information, and this has crucial bearing on a whole set of questions about the space of cyberspace that Benedikt raises and addresses later on: how big is cyberspace? What are its edges like? What shape is it? How are we to find our way around it? These four threads (and he notes there are many others) begin the process, then, that Benedikt picks up later, in his own contribution to *Cyberspace: First Steps*.

PROPOSING CYBERSPACE

'Cyberspace: some proposals' has a similarly speculative, future-facing tone, for which Benedikt is unapologetic; as he says at the start, there is vital work to be done at this stage: 'Before dedicating significant resources to creating cyberspace ... we should want to know how it might look, how we might get around it, and, most importantly, what we might usefully *do* there' (Benedikt 1991b: 119, emphasis in original). The project of envisaging cyberspace is crucial, therefore, and connects to the history lessons he has already taught us: to understand how we might think and build cyberspace, we need to understand how we have developed ways of acting in the world around us – phenomenologically, if you like (see p. 45). At times with vertiginous complexity, Benedikt talks us through the mathematics and cosmologies of space and time, speculating on the futures brought about by twin processes: 'the *etherealization* of the world we live in' and 'the *concretization* of the world we dream and think in' (ibid.: 124, emphasis in original). But before he can figure out cyberspace, he has to ask some tricky questions. First up: what is space?

Turning to mathematics and physics, and also to experience, he asks how we come to understand space both commonsensically and theoretically. How do we understand, experience and live in space and time, and how can this be fed into emerging cyberspace? What do we need to know about human spatiotemporal perception and use in order to build cyberspaces that work for, rather than against, their users? Benedikt, like Maria Bakardjieva who we shall meet in a while, is adamant that the views and experiences of 'ordinary users' are central to this task; otherwise, cyberspace will be inhospitable, alien, disorienting, useless.

Yet use must not be read to mean purely rational use or instrumental use. Remember thread one: symbolic storying, myth-making. Cyberspace must be magical, too – and it can be magical, Benedikt argues, through it violation of principles that govern our 'real life' experiences of space and time. As Sherry Turkle writes, cyberspace can be thought of as a liminal space, a space where rules are overturned (see p. 36 below). Prefiguring Turkle again, Benedikt discusses graphical user interfaces (GUIs) on computers as the beginnings of something, a new experience of space and time. But, for all his talk of violation, Benedikt is equally keen to establish some guiding principles for the design and building of cyberspace: principles aimed to produce usable, livable, but also magical worlds. These principles concern a number of key issues: the dimensions of space and cyberspace, how to visualize cyberspace, how to distinguish different 'data objects' in cyberspace, how 'things' will 'look' there, how we will find them, and so on.

The seven key principles of cyberspace design and build, according to Benedikt (and very roughly sketched here by me, to be selectively filled out later) are:

1   The Principle of Exclusion – two things cannot be in the same place at the same time;

2   The Principle of Maximal Exclusion – rules to minimize violations of the first principle, for example, over how 'big' and 'dense' cyberspace can become;

3   The Principle of Indifference – 'life goes on whether or not you are there' (ibid.: 160); cyberspace has an existence independent of users;

4   The Principle of Scale – the relationship between the amount of information in space and the amount of space in space;

5   The Principle of Transit – even through we may move instantaneously, travel as an experience is important, as is navigation;

6   The Principle of Personal Visibility – users in cyberspace should be seen, at some minimal level, by other users (but we should also be free to choose who is visible or invisible to us);

7   The Principle of Commonality – there needs to be an objective, shared social 'reality' in cyberspace, so that people see and hear the same things (at least partially).

Benedikt works through these principles, exploring how they might be realized in cyberspace. Some of his answers are intensely mathematical, concerned with modelling cyberspace in algebraic terms; others are (for me at least) more down-to-earth. For example, part of the riddle of the Principle of Maximal Exclusion is: how big does cyberspace have to be so that things there aren't in the same place at the same time too often? And once that problem occurs, how might cyberspace be expanded? The solutions to the latter quandary include literally making cyberspace bigger, producing a nested set of differently scaled cyberspaces, making data-objects multi-dimensional (so they might be in a different place or time at least in *some* dimensions), and so on. This is heady stuff, to be sure, a bit like imagining the size of the universe.

The question of the size of cyberspace is related by Benedikt to the question of how much data can it hold? How dense can that data become? How can we arrange data-objects so that users can comprehend them? And what do we want these data-objects to be like? Benedikt says, again recalling the magic dimension he is keen to retain in cyberspace, that some may be like mirages or rainbows, objects always far-off and elusive, but nevertheless clearly visible. Others will be fixed in place, objects we can move closer to, even 'touch'.

Of course, this isn't developing in a vacuum; users will enter cyberspace already 'hardwired' with a set of ways of dealing with space, time and objects. There's only so much magic we can take, before we get giddy, start suffering from 'sim sickness' (the disorientations experienced when VR makes us out-of-kilter). The task of producing 'workable data spaces' (ibid.: 150) must acknowledge and work with these features, balancing heady opportunities with limits and limitations. Benedikt offers a beautiful exemplification of this, again too long to quote in full, discussing an encounter in cyberspace with an 'unidentified flying data object' (UfdO). Nicely tinged by sci-fi, it is mind-boggling in its implications for the design and experience of cyberspace. Here, again, is my sketch: the user sees a UfdO in the distance moving at constant speed. The UfdO starts to slow down and shrink – has it turned to travel away from the user, or actually slowed and shrunk, or entered a denser area of cyberspace where it gets squashed and slowed down? How can the user tell?

The user tries to get closer to the UfdO, flying towards it, and, as the user does so, the UfdO gets larger and more detailed; only suddenly the user starts to decelerate, and cannot move closer to the UfdO – both have in fact entered a region of more space, expanded space, where everything is far away and travel takes a long, long time. (I know, so far, so *Star Trek*.) The point is that our perception of space, time, movement, objects etc. in cyberspace is going to have to cope with a lot more than we're accustomed to. I guess the question then becomes: how much do we think we *can* get accustomed to? What are the limits of the human in cyberspace, and can these be transcended, maybe by becoming posthuman?

This is part of the key paradox Benedikt has already hinted at: given that we can do pretty much anything in cyberspace, what *should* we do? Striking the right balance between the doable and the dreamable, between the real and the magical, is vital to the success of cyberspace development for Benedikt. So the Principles of Indifference, Transit and Personal Visibility, for example, don't simply map onto 'real life' experience. There is something extra in cyberspace, something that exceeds ordinary real life. I particularly like his discussion of the Principle of Transit, and therefore move to discuss this in more detail now.

POSTHUMAN

The idea that either (i) the human species is at an evolutionary dead-end, and must incorporate technologies in order to evolve to the 'next level'; or (ii) that we have long ceased to be human, because of our increasingly intimate relationships with nonhumans, such as technological artefacts. Often seen as similar to arguments about cyborgs (see p. 100), the idea of the posthuman provokes excitement in some, terror in others. It contains a number of variants in fields of biomedicine, science fiction and cyberculture theory.

MOVING IN CYBERSPACE

Setting aside the question of how the user might actually move in cyberspace – by flying or surfing, or by bouncing, seeping, slithering or strolling – Benedikt sets out some interesting ideas in the Principle of Transit, which he defines thus: 'travel between two points in cyberspace should occur phenomenally through all intervening points, no matter how fast (save with infinite speed), and should incur costs to the traveler proportional to some measure of distance' (Benedikt 1991b: 168). Toll roads on the information superhighway? Not exactly. Benedikt's concern is with the disappearance of the experience of travel – as an experience in itself – made possible by instantaneous communication. Zapping in a flash between places may be convenient, but it will be too disorienting for ourselves and for others. Moreover, being in multiple places at once, for Benedikt, needs some control, for much the same reasons. He suggests a limit on two or three 'clones' of oneself being present in cyberspace at any one time – a limit well exceeded only a few years later by the MUDders cycling through multiple personae, talked to by Sherry Turkle (see pp. 28–29).

But Gibsonian cyberspace is ripe with metaphors of movement through the 'datascape', and, given Benedikt's background in architecture, it is unsurprising that he would like to see cyberspace spatialized in ways that make travel something worthwhile. This is also about meeting fellow travellers – hence the Principle of Public Visibility is important because 'cyberspace must have a street life' (ibid.: 178). Travelling is about chance meetings, and also about the stories of journeys we can later retell. So Benedikt suggests that there should be both 'navigation data' and 'destination data' in cyberspace – because it is good to travel, but it's also good to arrive. Note that we still talk of *navigating* the web; as Benedikt says, the metaphor is one programmers and users both utilize in order to describe how they find their way around computers.

Now, remember that part of this Principle is about incurring 'cost'. Benedikt says this may be financial, just as long-distance phonecalls normally cost more than local ones, or it may be in terms of time: travel times may vary in cyberspace, partly as a result of your machine's processing power, but also as a way of making cyberspace seem 'spacey' – making things feel near or far. Distance is experienced as the time it takes to get somewhere, after all; Benedikt wants to put a brake on 'time–space compression' (see Castells, below) before they are compressed to nothing. He thus proposes a *landscape* for cyberspace, of routeways, ports of entry, virtual subway stations, and different modes of travel, from the speedy commute home to leisurely browsing. This range of spatiotemporalities is, you may have noticed, at odds with a key imperative of new technology: *faster, faster, faster!*

SEE YOU IN CYBERSPACE?

As already noted, this issue is related closely by Benedikt to his Principle of Personal Visibility – that we should, at some level, see and be seen in cyberspace. Who we see, he argues, should be a choice: 'I may want no self-styled teenage mutant dragon to leap into my view when he chooses to' (Benedikt 1991b: 179) – though he never really deals with the implicit issue of power here, other than to note that we might be able to invisibilize those we diagree with or dislike. Of course, many people are already invisibilized, by not being in cyberspace at all. But they are regrettably outside of Benedikt's thesis at this point. He is more concerned with the idea of balancing privacy and publicness in cyberspace (a theme picked up later, for example in Bakardjieva's work). Users should be prevented from 'cloaking' themselves, because visibility is linked to accountability – but also to vitality, in terms of the 'street life' of teeming hordes mixing in virtual cityscapes. Moreover, he points to a kind of virtual crowd behaviour – people will congregate, to see what's going on. This connects to Benedikt's seventh Principle, Commonality. People in the same cyberspace must have an overlapping shared reality, even if there can also be differences (magical ones). Otherwise communication is impossible, everyone seeing something different. But cyberspace will still have more flex in it, than 'real life', in terms of this commonality – it is a minimum, not a total condition.

Towards the end of the chapter, he turns to attempts to visualize the kinds of cyberspace he has been theorizing, making use of his own graduate students' work on databases and other virtual environments. (Castells and Haraway, discussed later, also make frequent, fully acknowledged, use of their students' work in this productive way.) He describes how a number of his students have responded to the task of building small-scale cyberspaces, for example to work as virtual slide libraries or video stores, or as 'data cells' in which immersive VR can be experienced. Importantly, these models stress the 'intuitive', hyper-linked ways of searching through databases, of navigating cyberspace, and thus of building cyberspace – a key theme discussed by the next two cyberculture theorists in this book, Sherry Turkle and Maria Bakardjieva.

Right towards the end of his discussion, Benedikt returns to a Gibsonian depiction of cyberspace, with flying data objects identified and unidentified, coasting above a vast urban plain – but a plain nevertheless with a horizon, and 'sky' above. In the sky waft travellers and traffic, plus data objects of various sorts, 'floating like ribbons, hot-air balloons, jelly-fish, clouds, but in wonderfully unlikely shapes' (ibid.: 205). He con-cedes, ultimately, that his chapter has been theoretical, some would say even speculative. But that has been his self-appointed task – a vital task, he rightly points out, in making some 'first steps' towards, and into, cyberspace and cyberculture:

> Let us begin to face the perplexities involved in making the unimaginable imag-inable and the imaginable real. Let the ancient project that is cyberspace continue.
>
> (Benedikt 1991c: 24)

Looking back on this work a decade later, Benedikt says in an interview that all he had imagined here has, in fact, failed to materialize:

> Cyberspace – that wonderful, phantasmagoric three-dimensional alternative reality imagined by William Gibson – was not actually shaping itself on-line as I and many others thought it surely would. ... To this day, only advanced intranet gamers have a foretaste of Gibsonian cyberspace: a real-time, shared, virtual space seamlessly mixing useful data, personal personae, and real-world, real-time connection.
>
> (Szeto 2002: 1)

Of course, this doesn't mean we don't have something called cyberspace, just that it hasn't taken the forms (and functions) that Benedikt (and indeed Gibson) foretold.

Benedikt does not explicitly talk of culture in his work here; apart from to note that there are cultural 'threads' to the history of cyberspace, and that this agenda is taken up by others in *Cyberspace: First Steps* (such as Stone 1991; Tomas 1991). Yet his two essays are profoundly cultural, in many ways: in their understanding of the role of symbolic stories in shaping cyberspace, in their insistence on an added magical dimension to cyberspace, in their discussion of uses and users. Hence my inclusion of Benedikt's prefiguring work as a key moment in cyberculture theory.

2 LIFE ON THE SCREEN

In his discussion of the three stages of cyberculture studies, already sketched, David Silver (2000) names Sherry Turkle's (1995) *Life on the Screen: Identity in the Age of the Internet* as one of the main pillars of the second stage, in which virtual communities and online identities become the main focus of discussion, and where the tone of that discussion is largely optimistic, stressing the possibilities offered by cyberspace to think and do identity and community anew. The book coincided, Silver adds, with transformations in the form and content of cyberspace, in its availability and accessibility, all of which 'helped to foster a less technical, more mainstream internet populace' (Silver 2000: 23). Turkle's book came out on the cusp of that change.

Sherry Turkle is Abby Rockerfeller Mauze Professor of Social Studies of Science and Technology at Massachusetts Institute of Technology (MIT), one of the powerhouses of cyberculture, where she is also Director of the MIT Initiative on Technology and Self (for a discussion of her life and work, see McCorduck 1996). Her work combines sociological and psychotherapeutic analysis – she is also a licensed clinical psychologist – and draws on a range of theoretical approaches and a huge amount of empirical material collected over many years. *Life on the Screen*, her third and best-known book, centres on what she calls the 'nascent culture of simulation', a culture she aligns with postmodernity, read through people interacting with computers: as she comments, computers are 'bringing postmodernism down to earth' (Turkle 1995: 268), providing many 'objects-to-think-with' for exploring the culture of the times and places she was writing from.

The book divides into three sections. The first, The Seductions of the Interface, focuses on forms of computer programming (and programmers), looking at the Macintosh interface as a new way for representing computing to users, and discussing the value of 'tinkering' as a way users come to understand their machines. Of Dreams and Beasts explores aspects of computer science's cultures, including artificial intelligence (AI) and artificial life (A-Life) – the key questions being what counts as thought, what counts as intelligence, and what counts as alive in contexts where these terms get blurry. Here, in one of the moves I particularly like in her work, Turkle observes and talks to children interacting with computers and 'computational toys' (see also Turkle 1998, 1999). The amazingly open and nuanced ways that kids talk about these objects-to-think-with provides many valuable insights into the future of human-machine inter-relationships. Finally, in On the Internet she discusses identity and community in virtual spaces, mainly MUDs (multi-user domains or dungeons). Talking with MUDders and participating in MUDding herself, Turkle explores ways that people using virtual spaces think about their self, or selves, and about how they connect or disconnect virtual life from 'real life' (RL). Deeply immersed in the cultures she studies – McCorduck (1996) says that her tone is almost confessional – Turkle has written a vivid portrait of what she saw as a 'liminal' period, a period of uncertainty, flux and change. While Silver is broadly right to see

Life on the Screen as enthusiastic about this period, I think there is more ambivalence in the book, itself arguably symptomatic of the time and place it was researched and written. And while it has inevitably dated, it retains a resonance despite the almost antique quality of some of the things Turkle discusses.

MUDs

Multi-user domains, dimensions or dungeons – are text-based games or environments in cyberspace. The word 'dungeon' hints at MUDs' origin as a computerized adaptation of the role-playing subculture Dungeons and Dragons – fantasy games in which players weave imagined worlds and take on characters to interact with each other in elaborate, long-running scenarios often drawing on imagery of swords and sorcery, goblins and wizards, castles and monsters. Early MUDs were written as on-line versions of these games, and many subsequent MUDs continued this 'adventure' or 'hack and slash' style. Others developed into 'social MUDs', not based around dungeons and dragons, but as virtual spaces for players (MUDders) to interact, adopting 'personae'. This interacting is known as MUDding. The spaces, characters and interactions were initially always text-based: players typed scenes, actions, talk, and this appeared on the screens of all players currently logged on. Social MUDs were often centred on a house or a town, with players adding new rooms or buildings. Since players can freely write their own personae, MUDs became associated with forms of identity play, such as gender switching – men adopting female personae on MUDs, etc. Some commentators saw this as potentially therapeutic, even political; others saw it as perpetuating gender stereotypes and as being potentially harmful. There was also much debate about whether MUDding represented a retreat from 'real life', and the subculture that grew up around MUDs was often seen negatively, as addicted to MUDding and withdrawn from reality. MUDs attracted a lot of academic attention, coming to be seen as key sites in cyberculture. Types of MUD have proliferated, and not all of them are solely text-based; there are graphic MUDs, and a proliferation of neologisms and acronyms, including MOOs, MUCKs and MUSHs.

LOOKING AT COMPUTERS

In her exploration of 'computational aesthetics', Turkle tracks a shift from 'modernist' computing, which saw the computer as a rational calculating machine and in which the computer was presented to us through the language of programming, to a newer, postmodernist computational aesthetic, embodied in the Mac, which instead presents us with the interface; or, more accurately, with the graphical user interface (GUI) – the things we see on screen. In place of lines of programming commands we see pictures (icons), buttons, things. Working a word-processing package, like the one I am using now for example, I see 'pages' that look like pieces of white A4 paper, and as I type the words form, their font and size and arrangement all sorted. What comes off a printer will look like what I now see on the screen, minus all the bits and bobs that encircle it (the buttons and so on). Turkle discusses this shift in aesthetic in terms of the computer's 'holding power', and she connects this interface aesthetic with how ordinary users relate to computers: where the earlier generations she studied in her previous book, *The Second Self* (1984), were either hobbyists seduced by the hardware and self-building ideals or hackers seduced by programming and a love of complexity, ordinary users want simplicity, don't want to know *how* things get done, only reassurance that they do get done: knowing *how to* make the computer work has replaced knowing how it works. This is key to the culture of simulation, which Turkle sees as having replaced the earlier culture of calculation. It impacts not only on our interactions with computers, but the way we conceptualize thinking, life, intelligence, the real and the virtual. While subsequent readings of the interface have criticized it for making users into idiots (see, for example, Fuller 2003; Stallabrass 1999), Turkle sees the interface as a fitting emblem of the times: 'the holding power of the Apple Macintosh, of simulation games, and of experiences in virtual communities derives from their ability to help us think through postmodernism. … Life on the screen carries theory' (Turkle 1995: 47, 49).

Indeed, Turkle peppers her book with theory, drawn from a wide range of sources, which she then connects cleanly to computing culture. She repeats time and again that life on the screen is a way of bringing postmodern theory down to earth, a way of showing how people are living the ideas she herself found hard to handle when exposed to them in what she calls her 'French lessons' – her encounters with the ideas of French theorists of postmodernism. But now those 'Gallic abstractions are more concrete' (ibid.: 15) – she has the objects-to-think-with for thinking about post-modern culture.

This alignment of computing and postmodernity is also worked through in her discussion of 'soft' programming styles – intuitive 'tinkering' rather than abstract reasoning. Using the web, for example, is about exploration, intuition, following leads, not knowing where you'll end up (or at least it was in the times Turkle was writing). There's something democratic in this, Turkle argues, in that access to computing has been broadened by user-friendly software that frees us from having to learn programming. She calls this a 'musical' culture of simulation, with computers 'more like harpsi-chords than hammers' (ibid.: 63) – still tools, but tools used in different, more open ways. Turkle finds the same approach in computer gaming, too. She watches kids playing games, talks to them about how they feel their way along, how they don't bother learning all the rules but prefer to get started and see what happens. She sees them ignoring things, working round things, playing the games how they want to. Out of all this observation and talk, she conceives three responses to the acknowledgement that we now inhabit a culture of simulation: resignation, denial and – the one she favours – using simulation to birth new forms of social criticism that 'would try to use sim-ulation as a means of consciousness-raising' (ibid.: 71), by making users think about simulations, virtual and real (see also Fuller 2003). Becoming 'simula-tion savvy' would give us ways to explore questions about what's real and what's simulated – and what's at stake in the way that distinction is made.

CY-DOUGH-PLASM

Today's children are growing up in the computer culture; all the rest of us are at best its naturalized citizens. ... [W]e can look to children to see what we are starting to think ourselves.

(Turkle 1995: 77)

Turkle's work with children is, for me, one of the most interesting areas of her research. She shows how children relate to and think about com-puters, computer games and 'computational toys' (e.g. virtual pets such as Tamagochi), and how they use play as a way to explore ideas about machine intelligence and 'aliveness'. Less encumbered by rigid ways of thinking than adults, children approach these questions playfully but also seriously. Looking at a series of studies over two decades, Turkle also sees shifts in the way children thought and talked about these 'intimate machines': what tools did they use to think them with? How did they conceptualize 'aliveness' – in terms of mobility, thinking, feelings? She writes that the children she worked with most recently seemed much clearer and more confident about drawing a distinction between themselves and machines, but that they had at the same time settled into a new way of understanding what machines can do and be: 'Now, children are comfortable with the idea that inanimate objects can both think and have a personality' (ibid.: 83). This shift parallels changes in the broader culture, around ideas of machine intelligence and ways of understanding human minds and bodies using machine metaphors.

She recounts watching 7-year-olds playing with Transformers – toys that can morph to take the form of people, machines or robots. She sees the children enjoying mixing up the transformations, leaving the toys half-changed, with a robot arm and human body for example. While some of the children protest that it isn't right to play with them like this, one girl says: 'It's okay to play with them when they are in-between. It's all the same stuff … just yucky computer cy-dough-plasm' (ibid.: 171). In their dealings with computer games that simulate life, in Transformer toys, in Speak 'n' Spell machines and in virtual pets, Turkle argues, children are 'pointing the way toward multiple theories in the presence of the artifacts of artificial life' (ibid.: 172). She lists a range of responses that the children she has worked with have made to computational toys and games, which is worth quoting at length for its exemplification of these multiple theories:

> My current collection of children's comments about the aliveness of what I have called A-Life objects (the Blind Watchmaker, Tierra, SimLife, mobots, and Lego-Logo robots) includes: The robots are in control but not alive, would be alive if they had bodies, are alive because they have bodies, would be alive if they had feelings, are alive the way insects are alive but not the way people are alive; the Tierrans are not alive because they are just in the computer, could be alive if

they got out of the computer, are alive until you turn off the computer and then they're dead, are not alive because nothing in the computer is real; the Sim creatures are not alive but almost-alive, would be alive if they spoke, would be alive if they traveled, are alive but not real, are not alive because they don't have babies, … [are] not alive because babies in the game don't have parents. … For all the objects, the term sort of alive comes up often.

(Turkle 1995: 172)

Now, this doesn't mean that these children are hopelessly confused, or dazzled by these machines into thinking they're alive; it shows us that ideas about life, intelligence, people and machines are rapidly, complexly changing. It offers an example of what Turkle refers to as cycling through, another key feature of the culture of simulation.

CYCLING THROUGH

Turkle uses the computing term 'cycling through' – running several different programs at once – to describe diverse experiences in the culture of simulation. Children playing with A-Life objects cycle through different ways of thinking and talking about the 'liveliness' of these new forms;

A-LIFE

Artificial life (A-Life) research centres on the replication of biological processes, behaviours and lifeforms in digital environments. A-Life focuses on evolution, replication, swarming behaviour, adaptation, etc. Some commentators argue that computer viruses can be thought of as A-Life forms. The particular forms Turkle discusses in *Life on the Screen* include **The Blind Watchmaker**, an evolution program that evolves 'biomorphs' through a process that mirrors natural selection (but is 'unnatural' because it is controlled by the programmer); **Tierra**, a program more closely simulating natural selection to let 'digital organisms' evolve through mutation (in their code); **Lego-Logo** robots built as computational toys using Lego blocks and programmed using Logo, a computer language; **SimLife**, part of the growing family of Sim games, which again lets players 'grow' lifeforms in their computers. These A-Life objects are linked by their underpinning emphasis on the idea of emergent intelligence: the lifeforms are programmed to evolve and to learn.

participants in MUDs move from real-life (RL) person to on-line persona or personae, cycling through different MUDs and between 'real' and 'virtual' worlds. Working on a computer using windows – boxed-off parts of the screen in which different programs and functions can operate – is also cycling through. Like the 1970s fad for split-screen TV, 'windowing' lets us keep an eye on a number of different things – a MUD, an email list, an accounts spreadsheet, a webcast – but also lets us focus primarily on one window, the one that occupies the majority of screenspace. We have grown accustomed to this way of working with computers, to clicking between screens, flitting between files and applications. And this experience has migrated out of computers, making RL just one more window, and letting us see ourselves as made of the windows we cycle through: 'windows have become a powerful metaphor for thinking about the self as a multiple, distributed system. ... In the culture of simulation, cycling through is coming to be the way we think about life itself' (Turkle 1995: 14, 174).

This experience is best exemplified for Turkle on MUDs. Reflecting the period in which it was researched and written, *Life on the Screen* spends a lot of time on MUDs, exploring how MUDders cycle through many selves, and how identity has thus become about multiplicity rather than unity; or, as Turkle titled an article in *Wired* magazine summarizing this part of the book, the key question here is 'Who am we?' (Turkle 1996). The postmodern self, theorized as fractured, fragmented, decentred, is the MUDding self, who types new identities in text-based virtual spaces, interacting with other identity-typists from anywhere and everywhere. MUDs are, Turkle says, a 'hybrid between computer programming and writing fiction' (Turkle 1995: 181), and they are, moreover, sites for writing and rewriting the self. (We might speculate that if she were writing this book today, she might have focused instead on weblogs.)

In the 'world of words' that makes up the MUD, participants (players) self-describe their adopted personae, and talk and interact with each other. This offers the opportunity for 'identity play' – for becoming someone else online. But that someone else needn't be thought of as a deceit; MUDs mix up this kind of thinking, asking where the 'real me' is, if indeed it exists at all: 'MUDs imply difference, multiplicity, heterogeneity, and fragmentation. … When each player can create many characters and participate in many games, the self is not only decentered but multiplied without limit' (ibid.: 185). Through extensive talk with players, and through participation, Turkle shows the different ways MUDs work as objects-to-think-identity-with. She raises the then-controversial issues of online deception and 'virtual rape', highlighting the costs of identity play in cyberspace. She also discusses the therapeutic potential of MUDs, asking whether they allow 'working through' or only 'acting out' of psychological issues. On the basis of her research, she is unsure how to call these questions, finding clear examples on both sides. But the MUDs she studied certainly provided a space to experience and experiment with the postmodern self, the self of the culture of simulation, the self that is cycling through different selves.

VIRTUAL SOCIETY?

After a long discussion of the self, Turkle turns to another topic that, in the mid-1990s, was generating a lot of heat about and in cyberspace: community. Her intervention in these debates explores, among other things, how RL and virtual life intersect and interact not only in terms of how individuals see themselves but in terms of how they see their 'fit' (or lack of fit) with the world around them. One particularly interesting aspect of this is her discussion of 'virtual social mobility' – how some of the people she talked to used things like MUDs to secure for themselves a virtual middle-class identity and status that they either lacked or had lost in real life. Some people used their programming skill or playing skill to gain status in MUDs, others simply reinvented themselves via their self-descriptions, and built up for themselves emblems of virtual status.

Turkle connects this phenomenon to a discussion of politics, finding some MUDders heavily involved in MUD politics but disengaged from RL politics, but also finding others using cyberspace as a grassroots political space and tool (see discussion of Castells below). MUDs can be an escape from RL, or a way of changing it. Here she worries about the potential for withdrawal from real life, and about issues of accountability and responsibility. While different people have such different understandings of the connection (or lack of connection) between life on- and off-line,

LIMINALITY

An anthropological concept, referring to movement between states or statuses, such as between childhood and adulthood, often involving a period of withdrawal from 'normal' society and the enactment of rituals – 'rites of passage' or pilgrimages. During the liminal phase, the 'normal' rules of society do not apply, and participants' identity and status are thereby erased to be made anew. In the anthropological model, the liminal stage is passed through, and the participants emerge out of the other side to be reintegrated into society with their new status and identity in place. For a critical discussion, see Hetherington (1998).

for example over whether being in a MUD is just play, or whether actions there have real repercussions, it is difficult to reach a consensus on such issues (indeed, consensus is intrinsically tricky in cycling through). Ultimately, Turkle sees virtual space as liminal: as a space of transformation or transition, where society's normal rules no longer apply, and from which new cultural symbols and meanings can emerge.

This sense of liminality, of the move towards the culture of simulation, pervades *Life on the Screen*, even though that in itself troubled the process of researching and writing it (McCorduck 1996). It is a book written at a time when 'we are dwellers on the threshold between the real and the virtual, unsure of our footing, inventing ourselves as we go along' (Turkle 1995: 10). But she is uncertain whether this liminal phase will ever pass, whether things can ever settle down again, or whether postmodernity means a kind of perpetual liminality. As a record of that moment, that dwelling on the threshold, *Life on the Screen* retains its importance and power as a landmark cyberculture text.

3 INTERNET SOCIETY

Maria Bakardjieva's *Internet Society: Everyday Life on the Internet*, published in 2005, is in many ways an exemplar both of Silver's (2000) 'critical cyberculture studies' and of Sterne's (1999) cultural studies approach to doing the Internet. It is promiscuous in its use of theory, as we shall see, and approaches cyberculture from a solidly empirical trajectory, informed by theory, and grounded in the practices of users. It therefore provides an excellent step-by-step guide to 'thinking the Internet' in particular contexts; so, while it doesn't tick all of Sterne's boxes in terms of a total study of cyberculture, it serves as a very good example of where we're at currently in terms of research and writing on cyberculture. It includes focus on a number of key aspects of cyberculture currently attracting a lot of attention – the material culture of the Internet, the 'everyday' uses to which it is put, issues of domestication, and the use of 'ethnographic' research (see also, among others, Hine 2000; Lally 2002; Miller and Slater 2000). While each of these aspects brings its own problems, they certainly work as a useful corrective to the perceived shortcomings of previous phases in the ongoing development of cyberculture studies.

Maria Bakardjieva is an assistant professor in the Faculty of Communication and Culture at the University of Calgary in Alberta, Canada. She went to Canada from Bulgaria to pursue postgraduate studies, and has also worked as a journalist. Her book is peppered with autobiographical (and 'autotechnographical') anecdotes, situating the bigger story she wants to tell in the very personal context of her own 'ordinary uses'. She describes the entry of computing into her own home, the process of coming to live with computers, or what Scannell (1996) calls the 'dailiness' of ordinary, everyday interactions on screen – her own, and those of her twenty-three respondents. This move towards the mundane, everyday dimensions of cyberculture is important and timely; as she remarks early on in the book, 'the practices of everyday users [have] remained largely invisible. The time to write this unglamorous, but nonetheless important, history was ripe' (Bakardjieva 2005: 5). Focusing on the dailiness or 'ordinari-ization' (Moseley 2000) of everyday cybercultures also led her to explore how online and off-line (or virtual and real) lives are folded together, in a move echoed in other work attempting to bridge the false divide between real and virtual life (see also Miller and Slater 2000). This is achieved both by talking to people and by observing their daily interactions in cyberspace – as well as the ways in which they have accommodated cyberspace in the space of the home, both materially (which room of the house is used for computers) and socially (who gets to go online, in what contexts, etc.). Drawing on a wide range of theoretical perspectives, which she mixes rigorously, Bakardjieva writes a richly detailed story of cyberculture's dailiness or everydayness.

Bakardjieva also has a desire to rewire the Internet to better suit the needs of everyday users – a large group previously neglected in studies that have instead focused on 'early adopters' as vanguards of a coming new technological age. She wants to ask, and answer, the question 'What should the Internet be like?' (Bakardjieva 2005: 6) – how are everyday users shaping cyberculture, in what ways can a focus on everyday uses be put to work in transforming the form and content of computers and cyberspace? Drawing on previous discussions of the politics of everyday life, such as the work of the French Marxist philosopher and sociologist Henri Lefebvre (1971, 1991), she calls for a programme of democratic Internet development responsive to, indeed informed by, 'ordinary' uses:

> The point is not to concoct utopian schemes for realizing the visions of theo-rists, technologists and political leaders, but rather to elaborate visions to be asserted in a technical and political process with an eye and ear turned to the unglamorous everyday initiatives of ordinary users.
>
> (Bakardjieva 2005: 193)

In one sense this programme represents a reclaiming of the democratic ideals of the 1960s computer counterculture, argued to have become lost in the rapid commercialization of cyberspace (see Abbate 2000). But those ideals also idealized the ordinary user and their ordinary uses;

HENRI LEFEBVRE

French sociologist and philosopher Henri Lefebvre (1903 – 91) extended Marx's ideas about alienation into the realm of everyday life, suggesting the need for the 'cri-tique of the real by the possible' as a way of remaking everyday life. Lefebvre's work proved influential in a number of disciplines, including human geography, where his *The Production of Space* (1974/1991) has been widely discussed; his work was also influential outside of academia: his *Critique of Everyday Life* (1974/1991) influenced the thinking of the political art activists the Situationist International, who similarly sought the re-enchantment of everyday life in the modern city, and whose actions are associated with the events in Paris of May 1968 (see p. 53).

Bakardjieva wants to start from a position of *knowing* the user, based on detailed empirical investigation.

THE ORDINARY USER

As Bakardjieva writes, the so-called ordinary user has been somewhat neglected in stories about technology, including computers and the Internet. This group is seen as passively receiving an already-developed technology, more or less enthusiastically or recalcitrantly, and then coming to accommodate it in their everyday routines. In the language of the social construction of technology (SCOT) approach, the technology arrives at the ordinary user already 'stabilized' – its form, uses and even meanings fixed, after a period of development and refinement in which other players had an input, but in which ordinary users were excluded. The technology is also 'black boxed' for ordinary users: they are not encouraged to 'look inside', to wonder how it works; they are told how to use it, and should accept that as sufficient.

Now, as should be apparent from my hint at Bakardjieva's desire to rewire cyberculture, this neglect of ordinary users is seen by her as wholly inadequate, and moreover as doing a disservice to ordinary users who, she argues, do much, much more than merely accept what lands in their lap. Moreover, home computers and the Internet exhibit, she suggests, a high degree of openness, especially when they become stitched into everyday life. Only by focusing on the dailiness of everyday uses can we begin to map out the contours of this openness and then use that map

SOCIAL CONSTRUCTION OF TECHNOLOGY (SCOT)

Part of the sociology of science and technology, SCOT shows how the 'shape' of technological artefacts is the outcome of social processes, such as the infuence of relevant social groups (for example, users). The form an artefact takes is ultimately stabilized only once the different relevant social groups have reached agreement. Thus the aim of the SCOT approach is to explore how different groups influence the development and final form of a technological artefact.

as the basis for rerouting the development of cyberculture towards more democratic and inclusive ends. To accomplish the task she has now set for herself, then, Bakardjieva assembles theoretical and methodological toolkits – in both cases reflecting Frow's and Morris's (2000) description of 'rigorous mixing' in cultural studies. She works through a number of theoretical approaches, critiquing each but also wanting to pick out their useful attributes, which she then connects together, letting them productively rub against each other. So, for example, she criticizes the SCOT perspective for its neglect of ordinary users, but holds onto its theorization of the mutual shaping of technology and society. She raids the nest of the critical theory of technology, appreciating its politics and its focus on thinking how things could be different, its emphasis on resistance. She locates Raymond Williams's (1974) *Television* in this approach, liking his focus on new patterns of cultural practice that new technologies help bring about. These practices – watching telly, surfing the net – loop back to inform the development of the technology, highlighting the productive role of users in shaping technological change.

Next in her sights is a focus on the meanings of technologies: how machines come to us coded in certain ways, reflected in their form and so on. As Donna Haraway puts it, machines are 'material-semiotic' entities (see pp. 120-1). Black boxing is an example of this coding, and Bakardjieva uses a favourite classic cultural studies theory, Stuart Hall's (1973) encoding / decoding, to talk about the ways in which producers seek to imprint certain meanings into the 'text' of the machine, but also how users can adopt a number of 'reading positions' as they decode those messages. As well as the preferred or dominant reading, where the user conforms with the encoded meaning, and where the user is said to be 'configured' by the machine to perform in accordance with its rules, users may also adopt resistant or negotiated reading or decoding positions. As Bakardjieva says, no matter how hard producers try to inscribe particular uses and meanings into their products, 'there remains an "irremediable ambiguity" about what the technology can do' (Bakardjieva 2005: 21) – sometimes referred to as the 'double life' of technology: the uses to which it is put that go beyond those 'written' into it. So the user isn't simply configured by the technology; there is a mutual configuring and reconfiguring. This is part of the process of domestication, viewed here as *relational*: it's about living with technologies, with work required on both sides – also seen later in the context of dog – human relationships in the work of Donna Haraway (see also Lehtonen 2003). But she is also critical of the way that domestication is viewed primarily as an act of consumption, preferring to see it as part of the ongoing production process: users are creative producers of new uses, new meanings and, particularly in the case of computing, new content, such as personal websites.

This point underscores her focus on 'users' rather than 'consumers' on the Internet, and also leads her in new theoretical directions, as she sees all the previous approaches sharing a 'repressive bond' by instating a separation between production and consumption, encoding and decoding, and so on (Bakardjieva 2005). Drawing on the ideas of French theorist Michel de Certeau (1984), she wants to think about technology as 'language': language is a system with normative rules and codes, but also has the openness to change, to new ways of talking, slang and word play. Now, de Certeau

ENCODING / DECODING

Cultural theorist Stuart Hall (1932 –), who came to Britain from the Caribbean in the early 1950s, developed the encoding / decoding model during his time at the Centre for Contemporary Cultural Studies at the University of Birmingham, UK. He proposed a new model of audience reception, looking at TV, in which the 'TV text' is seen as an articulation of linked but distinct moments of production, circulation, distribution and reproduction, and draws on the key idea of hegemony. Crucially, the model sees the TV audience as stratified, not homogeneous (for example, by class), and sees TV texts as 'polysemic' (carrying lots of different meanings) rather than being 'closed'. A particular set of messages may be encoded in a text by the various agencies responsible for its production, but the audience makes sense of the text's messages, drawing on their cultural context, experience, etc. So there are different reading or decoding possibilities: (i) dominant / preferred, in which the encoded message is accepted; (ii) negotiated – this position permits some disagreement but accepts the legitimacy of the hegemonic view; (iii) oppositional, which rejects the message encoded in the text and instead uses its own, contrary reading.

had already suggested using language as an analogy for the ways in which ordinary people exist within but also subvert rules and norms, using the example of walking in the city as the equivalent of speaking language. The walker is immersed in the city-as-system, walking its routes and following its rules, but he or she can improvise within that system, can skip or saunter, can walk with purpose or aimlessly. Use in technological systems is, Bakardjieva says, also analogous to speech (or walking). This idea is further developed by delving into linguistic theory, in particular the concept of 'little behaviour genres' – the different ways people talk in different situations, which we all carry round as a repertoire. How to speak to your mother, or your friends, or a shop assistant, or a dog – each type of situation has its own genre, and as we move to different social situations, so new ways of talking emerge.

Technology can play a crucial role here, of course: the telephone and later the mobile phone have their own genres of talking, and these are not preset by the technology but evolve through use. Bakardjieva adopts this idea to talk of 'use genres' in cyberculture: the ways we use the Internet has similarly evolved through the domestication of the technology, and we also use it differently in different social contexts (work or leisure, email or virtual shopping). Over time, some use genres 'stabilize' and become widely accepted – such as 'text speak' on SMS systems – whereas others fade to be replaced by new genres. In this way, Bakardjieva (2005: 31) suggests, use genres associated with technologies 'articulate technological change and social practice' (my emphasis), thus resolving the limitations

MICHEL DE CERTEAU

French sociologist and philosopher Michel de Certeau (1925 – 86) is best known for his work on everyday life and on popular culture as practice, which drew on historical and psychoanalytic theories. This work was concerned with understanding the structures of everyday life and the ways that ordinary people negotiate these, including their use of strategies (ways of appearing to conform to dominant social formations) and tactics (little acts of resistance that create spaces of freedom). Ordinary people were seen by de Certeau as 'tactical raiders' in their everyday practices.

she highlighted in other approaches to use (seen as consumption, etc.). Bakardjieva also highlights that new technologies interact with pre-existing use genres: they don't simply bring with them wholly new uses, but have to fit in with the ongoing evolution of uses and use genres. Hence some new technologies are taken up in unexpected or unprogrammed ways, while others flounder because their preconfigured use is at odds with current genres (3G phones being currently an example of the latter). That the computer still looks like a television and a typewriter reveals how technologies also bear the impress of previous uses, rather than being refitted to better suit current use genres – so there's still a lot of typing in cyberculture, even long after the invention of non-text-based uses. And a computer comes to us loaded with preset use genres, in the forms of programs, the interface, and so on. There are 'rules' we need to follow to make it work, yet the use genres to which we then put it are diverse and changing – as Turkle (1995) had already suggested in her discussion of 'tinkering'. For some people a computer is primarily a glorified typewriter (and even then, the things they type into it can vary immensely, from poetry to tax returns); for others it is a portal into virtual worlds (even if those worlds still demand some typing). Crucially, it is ordinary users who invent new use genres, and these are transmitted through the fabric of everyday life as 'users discover important, personally meaningful applications of the Internet' (Bakardjieva 2005: 117).

In her ethnographic work, then, Bakardjieva wanted to explore both the *a priori* rationalizations that users gave for getting connected to the Internet, and the relation between those rationalizations and the use genres they subsequently developed. Her typology of reasons for getting connected reads like symptoms of living in the network society: isolation, relocation or dislocation, job dissatisfaction or belonging to globally dispersed communities and networks (see also Bakardjieva and Smith 2001). Her respondents used the Internet to satisfy their perceived needs, whether for connection to events taking place in a now-remote 'homeland' or for communication with others suffering the same illness. These use genres reflect the social-biographical situations of the respondents, which Bakardjieva argues are typical of contemporary culture. But more importantly she sees the development of these use genres – which were not prefigured in the technology – as the creative engagement of ordinary users with the Internet, and as (potentially) empowering. What she calls the 'situated rationalities' of use (ibid.: 135) hint at a way to re-engineer the Internet as a democratic communication tool, and to resist its dominant stabilization as a tool of consumer capitalism. To accomplish this project necessitates the detailed exploration of use genres, therefore, in the situated context of particular users' everyday lives.

EVERYDAY CYBERLIFE

Hence it is important for Bakardjieva to also develop a tight theoretical view on what everyday life actually is. Luckily, she is aided here, too, by a bag of pre-existing ideas and theories, which she picks through to develop her own take of what some see as a peculiarly elusive concept (Highmore 2002). This is a similarly complex task, marshalling different perspectives and letting them rub up against one another. In her first encounter, phenomenological sociology meets Lefebvre's critical theory, and the idea of the lifeworld meets the idea of the everyday. The lifeworld – the spaces and times we inhabit and experience – provides a phenomenological framework for understanding a set of proximities and distances, or varying intensities, in all spheres of experience. Our decisions about what is relevant or meaningful to us relates to these 'zones': things most immediately around me, the tasks of today, are in a higher zone of relevance than more distant goals. Bakardjieva describes this in a nice autobiographical passage (which perfectly resonates with me here now, too):

> My situation at this moment is determined by the prioritized goal of producing a piece of text which paves the way towards completing my book and thus represents a miniscule component of my hierarchy of plans for the day, the year, and my life as a whole.
>
> (Bakardjieva 2005: 47)

This situation has both preset elements – writing books as part of academic work, etc. – and more open elements, such as the choice of what to write about, how to assemble arguments, and whose ideas to agree or disagree with.

Bakardjieva relates this neatly to the computer on which she is writing: it is now an expectation that academics can do word processing, so this is what she calls an imposed system of relevances, rather than a use she has openly chosen to make of her computer. But an hour earlier, she was online, on the same computer, chatting to some friends, making over her networked computer as 'an emotional, community-sustaining, social machine' (ibid.: 48). This ebb and flow of imposed and elective uses, or relevances, reveals the interplay of the lifeworld – in terms of both immediate situations and social-biographical situations – and the technology of networked computing. Mapping use genres onto social-biographical situations provides the bigger picture, therefore, of the 'significance the medium has acquired in society and culture at large' (ibid.: 50).

This lifeworld approach is then set alongside the Marxist critical theory of Lefebvre, who wanted to rescue everyday life from its co-option into capitalism. Crucially, where he concurred with Marx that work was an alienating experience under capitalism, he wanted to suggest that in the sphere of everyday life production could be unalienated, or disalienated – everyday life could be seen as the site where the self and the social world is produced, through what Lefebvre called the critique of the real by the possible, or what we might call thinking and doing everyday life otherwise. Lefebvre is useful to Bakardjieva for his attentiveness to the alienations of everyday life, and also to the disalienating, productive work of ordinary users. Synthesizing these two approaches, she thus sets out 'to study the Internet *from the standpoint of* and *for* ordinary users' (ibid.: 57, emphasis in original). To accomplish this she develops a

PHENOMENOLOGY

Literally the study of phenomena, phenomenology is the philosophical or sociological study of things as they appear in our experience or consciousness, and it seeks to explore the essential features of experience and the essence of what we experience, through studying conscious experience through the first-person, subjective point of view – the experience of the 'lifeworld'.

'critical phemonenology', drawing especially on the work of American 'post-phenomenologist' Don Ihde (1990), who proposed four types of human-technology relation:

- embodiment relations, for example spectacles, which are taken into bodily experience and which mediate the external world through improving the ability to see it;
- hermeneutic relations – technology represents the world, as in the case of a map (which needs the map reader's skill to 'see' the land-scape it represents);
- alterity relations, such as the feeling of a machine working against you, the machine being related to as if it is an animate 'other' (shouting at your computer for losing a file);
- background relations – things like lighting and heating which enable our lives but which we more-or-less take for granted (at least until there's a power cut or the boiler packs in).

Now, these relations can help us understand how something like the Internet works for ordinary users, how use genres develop. Ihde also discusses the dualism of amplification / reduction that new technologies bring: making some things easier, but also other things harder. New freedoms also bring new restrictions, and the ongoing negotiation of these has a bearing on the stabilization of use genres relative to both the immediate situation and the social-biographical situation of the user.

Now, to put some empirical flesh on this theorization, Bakardjieva decided to focus on the home, while also recognizing that home is not synonymous with everyday life. This focus represents a pragmatic move, to produce a manageable project that will still deliver on the big themes she is interested in. She understands the home as 'the place where objects from the exterior … are taken in and used' (Bakardjieva 2005: 73), but remember that for her use is not simply consumption, it is a productive act. She is interested in 'home-spun genres of using a new technology' (ibid.). So she goes to the homes of her respondents, including their 'electronic homes' (the places they inhabit in cyberspace), talks to them about their uses of the Internet, about the mundane dailiness of using net-worked computers.

AT HOME WITH (AND ON) THE INTERNET

As already noted, Bakardjieva wanted to explore how users decided that it was time to get the Internet at home. She also wanted to know how the getting of the Internet at home was realized, and how networked computing was incorporated into the lifeworlds of her respondents. For some, getting a home computer was about work, either in terms of the need to work at home, or in terms of job hunting or reskilling for a new career. Others expressed a vaguer intention, based on the perceived 'need' to be online, to keep up with current trends. They got the Internet because that's what you have to have, in a kind of deterministic take of the inevitability of technological 'progress' and the fear of being left behind. As one of Bakardjieva's respondents said: 'If you don't have it, you feel like an outcast. You don't know what is really going on. If you don't have email, who are you?' A third group got hand-me-downs, computers passed on by friends or relatives, so they got to use the technology because they had been given it, rather than having a prior perceived need. As she notes, this last group often suffered from low-grade out-dated machines that were poor performers in terms of Internet use – there is a 'digital divide' of users, let alone between users and non-users, based on the spec of their machines and connections. A lower-tech Internet, one that doesn't require the latest models and programs to use it, thus becomes part of Bakardjieva's democratic rewiring programme.

In her discussions with users about the process of getting connected and learning to use the Internet, Bakardjieva discusses the widespread help provided by 'warm experts'. In place of the often foreboding expertise offered through official channels such as help lines, her respondents often turned to more tech-savvy friends and relatives to help them out. In turn, users sometimes became warm experts as they mastered their own use genres. So, away from formal tuition and assistance, ordinary users deploy and receive warm expertise based on stabilized use genres and based on experience. Hence unauthorized use genres are passed on, like ways of speaking, even as the overall 'system' of use is preset by programming and so on. Like the debates about approaches to programming and like children's use of computational objects in Turkle's work, here users are seen experientially working within the system, each walking their own route through the 'streets' of cyberspace. As Bakardjieva (2005: 103) concludes, 'the particular category of everyday users produces its own culture of understanding and application of the medium'.

The category 'everyday users' also produces different stories, different ways of talking about the Internet, and different *feelings*: some respondents felt strong connection to their computers, others much less so. For some the computer was 'just a machine', while others enjoyed the tussle between the machine and their skill at using it. Bakardjieva refracts this back through Ihde's four-fold typology of human-technology relations, bullet-pointed above, but dropping the background relations:

- embodiment relations – the computer is an unobtrusive mediator between the user and the world (no need to understand how it works);
- hermeneutic relations – a focus on how the computer allowed them to relate to the world (for example, by understanding programming);
- alterity relations – the computer is a 'quasi-other', to be challenged and mastered, but also there is a clear relationship between the computer and the user.

As users settle in to life with the Internet, so they may change their orientations, and their feelings, in part as they experience the amplifications and reductions that the Internet brings (for example, the amplification in the amount of information available versus the reduction of being unable to judge its 'quality' or veracity). Becoming an Internet user, then, can follow many different paths and draw on different use genres. It also means making space and time for the Internet in the patterning of everyday life.

Drawing on previous work on the incorporation of 'media machines' into the home – such as Lynn Spigel's (1992) work on television (see also O'Sullivan 2005) – Bakardjieva looks at the 'microprocesses' by which room is made at home for the Internet. Like Elaine Lally's (2002) rich empirical work on home computers and Bernadette Flynn's (2003) discussion of the computer games console as a new 'digital hearth', a focal point for domestic life, Bakardjieva's study explores the mundane domestic material culture of technology – the networked computer as an object that has to be found a place in the arrangement of domestic objects in the rooms of the home – and also the accommodation of Internet use into the routines of everyday life: which household member uses it when? What uses are privileged? What other activities has Internet use replaced, and which has it enhanced? Placement and use are, in fact, woven together in an intricate geography of home Internet use genres.

Bakardjieva found some homes with a 'wired basement', the Internet installed in the cellar or basement under the house, a space ambivalently coded, sometimes as a male 'den', other times like a utility room. She found in some homes a battle for prime locations between the computer and the television, while in others the computer belonged in the home office, marking it as a work tool. Sometimes a spare room was used – a phenomenon often remarked upon by my own students, who complain that once they leave the family home to go to university, their parents quickly install a computer in what used to be the student's bedroom, making it over as a study. Placement was in some cases dictated by presumed use: a computer for play belongs in a room set aside for leisure, such as a sitting room; a computer meant for work belongs in an office. Multi-use networked computers mix up this tidy domestic geography, but rules of use (work more important than play) nevertheless structured the shifting meaning of the multi-use machine in the homes Bakardjieva studied.

There's something more at work here, though – something that Bakardjieva doesn't dwell on. The computer at home means different things to different people: for some it is a sign of the encroachment of work into the home, for others a window onto new and exciting possibilities, for yet others a sorry symptom of 'couch-potato' addiction to games and surfing. These feelings also clearly structure placement and use schedules. A friend who lives in a one-bedroom flat hates the fact that his computer 'looks at him' even when he's trying to relax, and I too for a long time refused to have a computer at home, because of its inevitable tie to work (see Bell 2001). And then there's the issue of children and the Internet, which Bakardjieva's respondents discuss – the need to have the computer in communal space so as to monitor children's use, versus encouraging children to freely explore cyberspace and become proficient in the warm expertise of use (both strategies of what Bakardjieva labels 'Internet parenting'). Of course, as Internet parenting shows, one key issue in letting the Internet into the home is its mixing of public and private, given both positive and negative spins by respondents. Crucially, everything that Bakardjieva describes going on in the homes of her respondents reinforces her view of active, productive work taking place as users make room in their everyday lives for the Internet.

The discussion of the mixing-up of public and private leads Bakardjieva into the vexed area of debates around 'virtual community' (see also Bakardjieva 2003). Here she develops another typology of ordinary users, on a continuum from 'infosumers' who have an instrumental view of the Internet, to those seeking to build communities based on far more than pure instrumental exchange. She wisely refuses to get mired in the debates about virtual versus real communities (see Bell 2001), instead talking of forms of 'togetherness'. In between her two poles lies a 'gradient of immediacy', with a balance between rationality and sociality, or we might say between facts and chats.

As with other elements of her discussion, Bakardjieva sees individual users as mobile on this continuum, their location dependent on both their immediate situation and their social-biographical situation. It is also dependent on a gradient between public and private, and movement in both directions as users reflexively manage their desire for publicness and privacy in cyberspace. Only the kind of careful, detailed study of Internet use advocated and exemplified by Bakardjieva can highlight how use genres map onto ideas of public and private as users craft relationships and boundaries. This point thus underlines her conclusion that 'the standpoint of users proves to be a crucial vantage point towards the present and future of the Internet' (Bakardjieva 2005: 195), leading her to call for user-centred research practice and for the development of platforms amenable to the use genres invented by ordinary users. As her last words in *Internet Society* evocatively summarize: 'everything is still at stake' (ibid.: 198).

SUMMARY

The three cyberculture theorists discussed here are all in some ways talking about different cyberspaces, and certainly different ways of understanding cyberspace and cyberculture, though there are common threads and echoes through their work. Benedikt, writing just ahead of the coming of cyberspace in the forms we know it today, flexed his architect's imagination to conjure the space of cyberspace as a Gibsonian cityscape, and he tied its current and future development to long histories of the evolution of World 3 – the world of abstract thought. Half a decade later, Sherry Turkle is fully immersed in an actual cyberspace, the space of MUDs but also of computational toys, of AI and A-Life; suddenly, cyberspace is taking shape in ways both like and unlike those predicted earlier. Also taking shape are the uses (and users) of cyberspace. By the time Maria Bakardjieva was researching and writing, cyberspace and cyberculture were both well-established World 3 phenomena, and well-established transdisciplinary fields of academic enquiry. Each phase of the development sketched here, every moment in cyberculture, is marked by its own concerns, hopes and fears, and by its own theories and methods. The next two chapters show how broad a field cyberculture has now become, yet how it is still possible to detect common ideas and common purpose.

WHY CASTELLS?

> We are entering, full speed, the Internet Galaxy in a state of informed
> bewilderment.
>
> (Castells 2001b: 4)

There are intentional ironies in the choices of theorists selected for more
detailed discussion in this little book. I doubt that either would wholly
recognize themselves in the tag 'cyberculture theorist'. As we have
already seen, the 'field' of cyberculture (or whatever) studies is diverse
and heterodox, too undisciplined to be called a discipline. But Castells is
even ambivalent about being fingered as a theorist; he insists that his work
proceeds from rigorous empirical inquiry, without the flourishes and
excesses of arch theory. In one essay that functions as a trailer for his most
important work, he states baldly that 'theory is simply a research tool'
before advocating 'disposable theory', that is the picking up and throwing
away of the bits and pieces that the writer offers up (Castells 2000b: 6).
Nevertheless, many critics agree that Castells has written one of 'the
most illuminating, imaginative and intellectually rigorous account[s] of
the major features and dynamics of the world today' (Webster 2002: 97),
a world imprinted in manifold ways with cyberculture; that is why
Castells.

Born in La Mancha, Spain, in 1942, Manuel Castells studied at the
University of Barcelona but left Spain in the early 1960s to escape the
Franco regime. He moved to France, studying at the Sorbonne and the
Ecole des Hautes Etudes en Sciences Sociales, where he worked on a doc-
torate under the supervision of Alain Touraine. He claims he 'accidentally
became an urban sociologist' when Touraine recruited him to a statistical

analysis of industrial location in metropolitan Paris (Castells and Ince 2003: 12). Following the completion of his doctorate on this topic, in 1967 he was appointed by the sociology department at the Nanterre campus of the University of Paris. He became involved in the May 1968 movement, which he describes as 'an extraordinary experience, one of the most beautiful of my life' (ibid.: 13). As a consequence of this involvement, however, he was caught by the police at a demonstration and expelled to Geneva. He then moved through academic jobs in Chile and Canada, then back to France (having been pardoned) from where he published his first book, *The Urban Question: A Marxist Approach* (1972).

After a number of visiting posts in the USA, in 1979 he became Professor of City and Regional Planning and Sociology at the University of California, Berkeley, from where he researched and wrote his influential study of his new home, San Francisco, *The City and the Grassroots: A Cross-Cultural Theory of Urban Social Movements* (1983). These books reflect a theoretical indebtedness to Marxism and to 'post-Marxist social science' (Webster 2002: 98), a lineage also reflected in his next major work, *The Informational City: Information Technology, Economic Restructuring, and the Urban – regional Process* (1989). Many of the themes developed in this book were further elaborated in the main focus of my discussion, Castells' three-volume *The Information Age: Economy, Society and Culture*, first published in 1996 – 8, with revised editions of two volumes

MAY 1968

A series of protests, strikes and demonstrations broke out across France in May 1968, arguably reaching almost revolutionary scale before being suppressed by the state. It began with student strikes in Paris, which escalated following police clampdowns, with widespread strikes by students and workers, eventually totalling some 10 million workers, or roughly two-thirds of the French workforce, and riots across the country. The government nearly collapsed, but order was restored over later months. The events of May 1968 have come to be seen as among the most significant near-'revolutions' of the last century, bringing together different socioeconomic groups protesting over a range of issues, both local and global. As such, May 1968 is an enduring emblem of left-wing radicalism.

appearing in 2000 and of the third in 2004 (for a full bibliography of Castells' work, see Castells and Ince 2003). Alongside his chair at Berkeley, Castells is also Professor of the Information Society at the Open Catalan University in Barcelona, and has held visiting positions at a number of other universities.

The fruit of more than a decade of research, and making extensive use of studies by his own doctoral students as well as enormous and varied empirical sources, *The Information Age* was also completed under the shadow of a cancer diagnosis with an initially pessimistic accompanying prognosis. As he puts it, 'I tried to put together, in a form as coherent as possible, everything I knew about everything, without limits, but with care, since these were [to be] my last words ... I brought information from many areas and from many corners, to give it away, to leave this world light of baggage' (Castells and Ince 2003: 149). Thankfully his health recovered, and the original plan to write a single volume was transformed into a trilogy, *The Rise of the Network Society* (1996a / 2000), *The Power of Identity* (1997/2004) and *End of Millennium* (1998/2000). It was written, he says, due to his frustration with available theories for explaining what he sees as a new society, the network society: 'I grew increasingly dissatisfied with the interpretations and theories, certainly including my own, that

MARXISM

Social theory and political practice based on the works of nineteenth-century German writer Karl Marx (1818 – 83), along with Fredrich Engels (1820 – 95). Marx developed a critique of society, most systematically in *Capital: A Critique of Political Economy* (1867). Marxism centres on the alienations caused by the capitalist system, which has at its 'base' a set of economic relations which are inherently exploitative of the working classes or proletariat. These relations favour the middle classes, or bourgeoisie. Working-class revolution is necessary to redress this exploitation. Marxism is both the political basis of forms of communism and a well-developed intellectual tradition, which has branched into different forms of Marxism, neo-Marxism and post-Marxism, and which has impacted significantly and enduringly upon the humanities and social sciences, as well as on the sphere of politics.

the social sciences were using to make sense of this new world' (Castells 2002 [1996]: 125). This three-volume book catapulted Castells to academic stardom: it has been favourably compared with landmarks in classical sociology, such as Weber's *Economy and Society* or Marx's *Das Kapital* (McGuigan 1999), and Castells has been labelled as definitely belonging to the 'sociological grand theory' tradition along with his mentor, Touraine, and writers such as Daniel Bell and Anthony Giddens (Stalder 1998).

Of course, this work has also attracted considerable critical commentary, much of it collected in Webster and Dimitriou (2004). Castells has continued a prodigious output of essays and commentaries further developing the key themes of *The Information Age*, for example in the lectures published as *The Internet Galaxy: Reflections on the Internet, Business, and Society* (2001b). I want to summarize the trilogy here, before isolating and discussing more fully a number of (to my mind) the most important insights and ideas presented in *The Information Age* and its constellation of related writings.

A SKETCH OF THE INFORMATION AGE

Let's start at the end, the end of *The End of Millennium*, where Castells summarizes the main spine of his argument:

> A new world is taking shape in this end of millennium. It originated in historical coincidence, around the late 1960s and mid-1970s, of three *independent* processes: the information technology revolution; the economic crisis of both capitalism and statism, and their subsequent restructuring; and the blooming of cultural social movements, such as libertarianism, human rights, feminism, and environmentalism. The interaction between these processes, and the reactions they triggered, brought into being a new dominant social structure, the network society; a new economy, the informational / global economy; and a new culture, the culture of real virtuality.
>
> (Castells 1998: 336, emphasis in original)

Here, in a rather lengthy nutshell, is Castells' thesis: the birth of a new world, and a new social morphology and social structure, resulting from three major, serendipitous but independent (at least initially) occurrences.

The task he sets himself in *The Information Age* is therefore to explore and to account for these processes and their outcomes, many of which he had already begun to chart in *The Informational City*. As the subtitle to the trilogy suggests, Castells tracks this through the interconnected domains of economy, society and culture, marshalling huge banks of empirical data to illustrate his argument and convince his readers of its veracity. And it is convincing; Jim McGuigan (1999: 104) calls the book 'a truly remarkable scholarly achievement, bringing together enormous amounts of data in a coherent analytical framework' as well as noting that it is also 'a political intervention of strategic importance'.

To map out the contours of this new world, the book divides into three volumes, as already noted. The first, *The Rise of the Network Society*, delineates what Felix Stalder (1998: 303) labels 'the structural aspects of the Information Age that have created the Network Society'; the book covers economic globalization, 'informationalism' and the 'informational mode of development', two key concepts; changes in work patterns, the impacts of new media or multimedia on information and communication; and the restructuring of space and time into, respectively, the 'space of flows' and 'timeless time'.

The Power of Identity explores responses to the network society in terms of cultural social movements. Castells argues that it is at the level of cultural identity that political resistance to the dominating powers of global informational capitalism is worked through, often in what he calls 'cultural communes' in which groups build alternative lifestyles and worldviews. The increasing use of the Internet as a site to do 'identity work' is revisited here. He draws on recent theorizations of social identity that highlight the social construction of identity, and he identifies three broad types of identity: legitimizing, resistant and project identities. The first can be thought of in the more 'traditional' sense of citizenship and rights, the second exemplified by fundamentalisms, and the third can be understood as akin to Giddens' (1991) notion of reflexive self-identity, of identity as a project upon which one works, unendingly. To elucidate, he explores manifestations of these forms of identity in diverse sites, including religious fundamentalism, nationalist and secessionist movements, guerilla and terrorist groups such as the Zapatistas, Aum Shinrikyo (and, in the 2004 edition, al-Qaeda); the environmental, feminist and lesbian and gay movements (associated in Castells' argument with the end of 'patriarchalism'); the changing role of the nation-state as a source of identity; and the role of the media in transforming politics (and therefore political identifications).

End of Millennium rounds off the trilogy with what Stalder (1998: 306) with some accuracy calls 'a somewhat eclectic mix of major events or trends', including the collapse of Soviet statism, the rise of the Fourth World, also known as the black holes of informational capitalism (with explorations of its manifestations in Africa, in the USA, and in terms of the exploitation of children); a discussion of the rise of Pacific Rim economies and of European integration; and, the part of the volume that attracted most attention, his focus on the global criminal economy as the 'perverse' face of global capitalism – networked, organized, transnational crime, including the trafficking of various things: drugs, weapons, nuclear material, people, body parts, and money. Drawing on powerful localized identifications (gangs, cartels, etc.) but networking globally in strategic alliances, 'criminal networks are probably in advance of multinational corporations in their decisive ability to combine local identity and global business' (Castells 1998: 204). The volume ends with a conclusion to the trilogy, 'Making Sense of Our World', which revisits the restructuring effects of global informational capitalism, for example in terms of class, in terms of social exclusion, and in terms of the tension, or dialectic, between the net and the self, or between the network society and the power of identity: 'on the one hand, networks of instrumentality, powered by new information technologies. On the other hand, the power of identity, anchoring people's minds in their history, their geography, and cultures. In between lies the crisis of institutions and the painful process of their reconstruction' (Castells and Ince 2003: 150). In an uncharacteristically futurological finale (elsewhere Castells professes an allergy to futurology), we find the author seeing things getting worse but also some glimmers of hope, through a list of 'ifs'.

Clustering around the trilogy are related publications, papers, interviews, reviews and comments (see Further reading for resources). *The Internet Galaxy* (Castells 2001b), a kind of sequel, revisits some key themes of *The Information Age*, but with a more explicit and sustained focus on the Internet, since Castells (2001b: 6) sees it as 'particularly susceptible to intensifying the contradictory trends present in our world' whether in terms of e-business, networked social movements, or the digital divide. In the second edition of the trilogy, too, the Internet figures more centrally, reflecting Castells' willingness to revise his thesis as things move on – though he reminds us that the network society means more than just the Net.

CASTELLS' KEY IDEAS

1 NETWORK SOCIETY

> This information age has never been a technological matter. It has always been a matter of social transformation, a process of social change in which technology is an element that is inseparable from social, economic, cultural and political trends.
>
> (Castells with Catterall 2001: 3)

In order to fully grasp the forms and functions of the network society, we need to attend to the theoretical building blocks and witness the moves that Castells makes in assembling his argument. These are extensively elaborated in *The Rise of the Network Society* (1996/2000) and succinctly summarized in a series of articles (see especially Castells 2000b, 2001a, 2002 [1996]).

INFORMATIONALISM

First is the concept of informationalism, which Castells uses to delineate a new economic system and era, preferring the term over other epoch-definers such as 'post-industrialism'. He also prefers to think of the transition to an informational economy in terms of a socio-technical 'paradigm shift' rather than a revolution (Castells 2001a). As global competitiveness (of

CAPITALISM

An economic system in which the means of production are owned and controlled privately, labour is exchanged for wages, and the production, distribution and pricing of goods and services are determined by supply and demand in a market context, rather than by the state. Those in control of the means of production generally run them for profit, which is appropriated by the owners of capital – the capitalists. Capitalism contrasts with socialism or communism, where the means of production and the commodities produced are owned and used by the state or collectively. An economy with a large amount of state intervention combined with capitalist characteristics is often referred to as a mixed economy and, if state intervention is dominant, as statism.

workers, corporations, states) increasingly depends on access to and ability to manipulate information, so we have a new economy: 'in the new, informational mode of development the source of productivity lies in the technology of knowledge generation, information processing, and symbol communication. ... [T]he action of knowledge upon knowledge itself [is] the main source of productivity' (Castells 1996a: 17). As Webster and Robins (1998) put it, this entails a shift in production from hardware to software and to data. And given the fatal collapse of statism (communism), we have in fact entered the age of global informational *capitalism*, which Castells only half-jokingly names 'a new brand of capitalism' (Castells 2000a: 52).

At the heart of informationalism is what Castells refers to as the informational mode of development, a term he uses to distinguish what's changed in this new economy: we are still in a capitalist mode of production, in terms of the relations between capital, property ownership and labour (even if, as we shall see, he argues that the social structure, i.e. class, has fundamentally changed). Following his old mentor, Alain Touraine, he specifies a mode of development as 'the technological arrangements through which humans act upon matter (nature), upon themselves, and upon other humans' in order to generate wealth (Castells 2000b: 9). Modes of development are defined, he adds, 'by their central technological paradigm and by their principle of performance' (ibid.), hence the shift from an industrial to an informational mode of development: wealth is now created, under a capitalist mode of production, through the action of knowledge upon knowledge. Here is how Castells lays out the bigger picture:

> The emergence of a new technological paradigm organized around new, more powerful, and more flexible information technologies makes it possible for information itself to become the product of the production process. To be more precise: the products of new information technology industries are information-producing devices or information processing itself. New information technologies, by transforming the processes of information processing, act upon all domains of human activity, and make it possible to establish endless connections between different domains, as well as between different elements and agents of such activities. A networked, deeply interdependent economy emerges that becomes increasingly able to apply its process in technology, knowledge, and management to technology, knowledge, and management themselves.
>
> (Castells 1996a: 67)

So the economy is informational, its elements are deeply interdependent, and it is also global: this does not equate to a 'world economy', but means that we now have an economic system 'whose core, strategically dominant activities have the potential of working as a unit in real time on a planetary scale' (Castells 2002 [1996]: 126) – exemplars include financial markets and multinational corporations.

Financial globalization, which Castells concentrates his sights on for a long time and which he sees as 'the major structure of domination in our world today' (Castells with Catterall 2001: 29), has become so disembedded and disconnected from 'the ground' that it functions almost autonomously; Castells refers to it, in one of his rare *tech-noir* moments, as the Automaton:

> We have created an Automaton, at the core of our economies, decisively conditioning our lives. Humankind's nightmare of seeing our machines taking control of our world seems on the edge of becoming reality – not in the form of robots that eliminate jobs or government computers that police our lives, but as an electronically based system of financial transactions.
>
> (Castells 2000a: 56)

This Automaton, which he also refers to as a faceless 'collective capitalist', is not just a robotized market, however; its logic is more complex

and chaotic, even random – the financial system is marked by 'information turbulences', unforeseen booms and busts, such as those around so-
called dot.com businesses. The chaotic dynamics of the global economy,
moreover, can make their effects felt anywhere and everywhere, purpo-
sively or incidentally, even though large parts of the world are formally
excluded from its operations. Castells refers to these excluded regions as
the Fourth World, places skipped over or stripped out by global finanscapes (Appadurai 1990). As Castells makes clear, this new economy has a
profoundly uneven cartography (but with what he calls an enduring
architecture): 'the global economy emerging from informational-based
production and competition is characterized by its *interdependence*, its
asymmetry, its *regionalization*, the *increasing diversification within each region*,
its *selective inclusiveness*, its *exclusionary segmentation*, and, as a result of all
these features, an extraordinarily *variable geometry* that tends to dissolve
historical, economic geography' (Castells 1996a: 106, emphasis in original). These features are manifest at a variety of spatial scales, from
nation-states to regions, organizations to workers.

APPADURAI'S SCAPES

According to anthropologist Arjun Appadurai (1990), the new global cultural economy is characterized by disjunctive flows, or 'scapes'. He identified five:

- ethnoscapes – flows of *people*: migrants, refugees, tourists, guest workers –
  moving individually or collectively, permanently or temporarily, voluntarily or
  involuntarily
- technoscapes – flows of *machinery*: mechanical and informational, low tech
  and high tech, including technical skills
- finanscapes – flows of *money* or capital – both legitimate and illicit, global
  stock markets and money laundering
- mediascapes – flows of *images*: capabilities to produce and disseminate
  media 'texts', or what Appadurai calls 'image-centred, narrative-based
  accounts of strips of reality' that take on different meanings depending on
  where they are consumed
- deoscapes – flows of *ideas* or ideologies: especially the globalization of
  Western metanarratives such as democracy, freedom, human rights, etc.

NETWORKING

So, this new economy requires new ways of working, too, embodied for Castells in the network enterprise and the networker (someone who works by networking, and also who works in the net). The network enterprise is a flexible arrangement suitable to the needs of informational capitalism; it is defined by the networking logic with its antecedents in the crisis of capitalism, which was partly resolved by restructuring how business organizations work (as well as by extensive deregulation). So-called post-Fordist flexible specialization replaced Fordist mass production; new work cultures emphasized worker autonomy and multitasking ('Toyotism'); the small firm became a role model for entrepreneurialism and 'enterprise culture'; and ultimately the network enterprise emerged as the ideal organizational form – a flexible association of components, or nodes, that is never still, but changes from project to project: 'networks are the fundamental stuff of which new organizations are and will be made' (Castells 1996a: 168). States, too, begin to look like networks, either by devolving to regions or by linking up strategically in international pacts, with other states and with organizations. Networks are horizontal, non-hierarchical, fluid and mobile, and their unit of work is the project.

The flexible structure of the network is governed by the simplest binary logic: on or off, inclusion or exclusion: networks are 'value-free. They can equally kiss or kill: nothing personal. It all depends on the goals of a given network and on its most elegant, economical, and self-reproductive form to perform these goals' (Castells 2001a: 167). So, what is the impact of the network form of business organization on patterns and experiences of

POSTINDUSTRIALISM

Describes shifts in the economy and society as they move from a manufacturing industrial base towards service, knowledge and information sectors. Associated with sociologist Daniel Bell's (1974) *The Coming of the Post-industrial Society*, the concept has blurred into other, related notions such as post-Fordism and flexible specialization, all of which describe the political, social, economic and spatial transformations brought about by the decline in the economic importance of manufacturing and its effects on relations of production and consumption.

employment? Basically the same binary logic: in or out, switched on or switched off. There is a new (Castells says newest) division of labour in the global informational economy, with four different types or classes of labour: 'the producers of *high value*, based on informational labor; the producers of *high volume*, based on lower-cost labor; the producers of *raw materials*, based on natural endowments; and the *redundant producers*, reduced to devalued labor' (Castells 1996a: 147, my emphasis). At the same time, and potentially adding confusion, Castells says that there are three positions available in the new global occupational structure, which he labels networkers, jobless and flextimers.

The language used to describe the new world of work is familiar from 'management speak': downsizing, delayering, multitasking, outsourcing, subcontracting, portfolio careers – all euphemisms for the dramatic changes in the organization of work in this new economy that have brought new insecurities and anxieties for many. The lucky ones get to be 'networkers' at the top of the pile. Whole labour forces meanwhile can be 'switched off', bypassed, routed round: as Castells puts it, capital is global but this labour is local, unlike the footloose nomads of the transnational service class, the networkers. De-unionization, casualization, marketization, individualization, feminization – these are the fates facing flextimers hoping not to be switched off.

Flextimers are often casually employed on a contract-by-contract basis, negotiated via agencies: thus they lack security of employment and attendant benefits; they are required to 'flex' their time, to work in patterns suited to the needs of their employers, who may pay them piece rates and who 'incentivize' productivity through surveillance; they are often underemployed, working part-time. Often this kind of work recruits female labour; as Castells (2001a: 171) observes, 'the organization man [is] now replaced by the flexible woman'. This group, who Castells also labels 'generic labour', is seen as disposable, replaceable either with more compliant human labour from somewhere else, or by even more compliant nonhuman labour in the form of automation. These workers are networked rather than networkers, and can be seen and treated as little more than 'human robots' (Castells 1996a: 244). So there is a 'stepped up division of labour' with, on the one hand, 'self-programmable labour' – networkers well equipped to adapt to the demands of the flexible information workplace; and, on the other, 'generic labour', exchangeable and disposable. Further beyond that there are 'legions of discarded, devalued people [who] form the growing planet of the irrelevant' and whose only entry into global info-capitalism is through the 'perverse connections' of the global criminal economy (Castells 2000b: 12).

NETWORK CULTURE

Castells spends a fair amount of time analysing the work and life patterns of networkers, joining a lineage of scholars seeking to understand these new transnational, cosmopolitan technocratic - financial - managerial nomads (Webster 2002). The characteristics of this top strata of 'informational labour', seen by Castells and other commentators as powering the new economy and comprising the 'collective capitalist', include their 'foot-looseness' – they feel no sense of rootedness to particular places, no strong sense of local or national identity, nor any 'organizational identity' based on belonging to a particular firm. They have highly transferable skills, enabling them to adapt quickly and smoothly to ever-changing networks and projects – they can, in management parlance, multitask (remember that Castells calls them 'self-programmable labour'; they don't need training or reskilling, because they constantly upskill themselves). They are not white collar, but, as Andrew Ross (2003) puts it, 'no collar' – casual in attire and attitude, but deadly serious about their work. They are as restless as the flows of the financial markets, yet they are still concentrated in major metropolitan centres, where they carve out cosmopolitan lifestyles through their consumption practices. They live in key nodes of what Castells calls the 'space of flows' (see below).

There exists, Castells argues, a worldwide network of exclusive enclaves, which comprise the habitat of this elite: boutique hotels and loft apartments, VIP lounges at airports, exclusive restaurants, personal trainers, high-culture events. Castells is even able to cartoon the components of this group's lifestyle:

> the regular use of spa installations (even when traveling), and the practice of jogging; the mandatory diet of grilled salmon and green salad, with *udon* and *sashimi* providing a Japanese functional equivalent; the 'pale chamois' wall color intended to create the cozy atmosphere of the inner space; the ubiquitous

laptop computer; the combination of business suits and sportswear; the unisex
dressing style; and so on.

(Castells 1996a: 417)

As we shall see, this group has made its mark on the cities it inhabits or
passes through, too, in terms of new building types and architectural and
interior styles that are serially reproduced to make these nomads feel
(temporarily) at home, wherever they land.

Now, there is a further important dimension to add to the mix here:
what is the defining work ethic of the new information economy? What,
Castells asks, glues together the networks of networkers? Unsurprisingly,
he names it, in an echo of Max Weber, the spirit of informationalism. Here
Castells begins to formulate ideas about the culture of the network society,
first off in terms of its organizational codes: it is, he says, 'a culture of the
ephemeral, a culture of each strategic decision, a patchwork of experiences and interests, rather than a charter of rights and obligations. It is a
multifaceted, virtual culture' (Castells 1996a: 199, emphasis in original).

BEYOND THE NETWORK

On the periphery of and outside these networks, as we have seen, there
are other workers, unable to share in this virtual culture or to surf through
the space of flows. The duality between the two positions is stark, Castells
argues, and becoming ever starker: 'extraordinary creativity and extraordinary social inequality and social exclusion are going hand in hand'
(Castells with Catterall 2001: 4). What (limited) options are available to
those switched-off populations unable to reap the benefits of the network
society? One option, as we have already seen, is to participate in the 'perverse connections' of the global criminal economy, to patch in to other
networks that work with the same logic but with very different means
and ends. Another is withdrawal, retreat into what Castells calls 'cultural
communes' built around assorted fundamentalisms: 'there is life beyond
the network society: in the fundamentalist cultural communes that reject
dominant values and build autonomously the sources of their own
meaning; sometimes around self-constructed alternative utopias; more
often, around the transcendent truths of God, Nation, Family, Ethnicity,
and Territoriality' (Castells 2001a: 170).

In addition, there are possibilities to appropriate the network society, to make its logic work for other ends, in a process Castells (1999) calls 'grassrooting the space of flows' in echo of his earlier work on social movements. These movements may intersect in complex ways with the space of flows, with the global criminal economy, and with cultural communes, as his studies of the American patriot movement, Aum Shinrikyo, the Zapatistas, al-Qaeda, the anti-globalization and green movements, and feminist and lesbian and gay politics all show in different ways (Castells 1997/2004). But Castells is overall quite sanguine about this new social morphology: 'a society made up of the juxtaposition of flows and tribes ceases to be a society', he writes (Castells 1996b: 31), noting that social movements can be regressive as well as progressive – qualifying his earlier statement that social movements were the only remaining engines of social change in the network society (see also Castells and Ince 2003). But this position is seen as fatalistic by some critics, in that it suggests that global informational capitalism has 'won' and has 'switched off' any alternatives (Webster and Robins 1998). He has continued to work over this part of his analysis, but his final view on the grassroots seems ambivalent.

NETWORK SELF

In *The Internet Galaxy*, Castells ponders some more the 'society' in network society, siding with those researchers and critics who see the 'social reality' of the Internet, in terms of users' participation, as 'an extension of life as it is, in all its dimensions, and with all its modalities' (Castells 2001b: 118). Reviewing the available evidence, and not believing the hype, he ends up ambivalent here, too, about the effects of Internet use on social relations and sociability, even while he sees sociability being transformed off-line. However, his reading of online social interaction leads him to formulate the idea of 'networked individualism', noting that virtual communities are 'me-centered networks' or 'personalized communities' wherein sociability is 'privatized' (ibid.:128; see also Wellman and Haythornthwaite 2002). As noted above, the expanding and proliferating platforms for individuals to produce and consume (or 'prosume') mediated reflections of self-identity, from blogging to podcasting to on-line gambling (see below), provide endless opportunities for the exercise of networked individualism. Moreover, this individualism, Castells argues, is the result of the network society as sketched above: it is the outcome of the individualization of work in the network enterprise, of the decline of patriarchalism, of withdrawal from politics and civil society, and of new patterns of urbanization and the dislocation of the spaces of everyday life in cities cut through by flows (see below). Individuals caught in the space of flows become networks themselves, and networked individualism becomes the new social pattern (Castells is keen to stress this is not merely a collection of isolated individuals). This is in some ways a transformation of his earlier discussion of the dialectic, even conflict, between the net and the self (e.g. Castells 1996a / 2000); here the net *is* the self, and people have assembled 'portfolios of sociability' to match their portfolio careers, 'project identities' to match their project-based work lives: 'the construction / reconstruction of the self is tantamount to managing the changing set of flows and codes that people are confronted with in their daily existence' (Castells 1996b: 34). Or, as he puts it in an autobiographical aside, 'I am afraid I look more like a flow' (Castells 1996a / 2000: 243).

SUMMARY

The network society has a number of distinguishing features, though critics are unsure just how 'new' this all is (Castells says the question of newness is boring). We are now living under the condition of global informational capitalism, brought about by three independent processes: the information technology 'revolution', the crisis and restructuring of capitalism and statism, and the rise of new social movements. Out of this whirl of change come the network society and the network logic. The global economy is chaotic and turbulent, and seems to function autonomously, with very variable impacts around the world. There is a new spatial division of labour, based around self-programmable elite labour, replaceable generic labour, and the discarded jobless. Working now means networking, and organizations become network enterprises while individuals develop portfolio careers or risk being switched off. The elites of self-programmable labour live exclusive lifestyles while social exclusion and poverty escalate around them; the poor and excluded react by joining the global criminal networks, or by withdrawing into fundamentalisms. Networking logic extends to the self, either by counterposing the net and the self or through network individualism, though grassrooting offers ways to bring together the net and the self, through the networking of project identities.

2 SPACE OF FLOWS

Castells says that his concept of the space of flows is very important and very complex, even counter-intuitive. First elaborated in *The Informational City*, it is one area of *The Rise of the Network Society* where he permits himself a more theoretical approach (and later even admits to previous theoretical mistakes; see Castells and Ince 2003). Based on the observation that 'dominant functions were increasingly operating on the basis of exchanges between electronic circuits linking up information systems in different locations', Castells' central premise is the dichotomy between the space of flows and the space of places as the geographical manifestations of the network society (Castells 2002 [1996]: 131). The space of flows is woven closely together with his idea of 'timeless time', which I also discuss in this section.

NETWORKS AND FLOWS

The notion of flows is integral to the idea of the network: 'the space of flows is the material organization of time-sharing social practices that work through flows' (Castells 2002 [1996]: 132). The network is a series of points, hubs or nodes – these can be people, cities, businesses, nation-states – connected together by flows of various sorts: flows of information, of materials, of money, of people. So the space of flows is both the nodes and the connecting flows. Hence part of its complexity. Now, the idea of global flows had already been discussed lucidly by Arjun Appadurai (1990), who is not referred to by Castells but whose ideas nevertheless have a striking resemblance. Trying to think about globalization, Appadurai conceptualized the world being criss-crossed by a series of disjunctive or non-isomorphic flows (see p. 62). He listed five, and gave each the suffix -scape, to conjure images of a landscape, all hills and valleys, humps and bumps: ethnoscapes, finanscapes, technoscapes, ideoscapes and medias-capes (respectively, flows of people, money, technology and skill, ideologies, and media texts). These flows are chaotic, varying in speed and intensity, overlapping, attracting or repelling one another. Moreover, they don't merely circle the globe like satellites; they land. Where they land, and what results from their landing, is similarly unpredictable (even though there are patterns and there is stability in parts). Where they land are the nodes in the network. But there are different kinds of nodes, some with greater capacity to control at least some flows, for example by refusing entry to some people, or blocking some media content from being accessible. 'Strong' nodes can act as magnets, drawing down some flows while also pushing others away, deflecting them elsewhere. Other nodes are relatively powerless, and are endlessly buffeted and battered as flows land. Appadurai and Castells concur that the nodes where these complex processes are most vividly at play are so-called global cities, as we shall see.

Another characteristic of the space of flows relates to time: time is morphed by the space of flows, creating what Castells calls timeless time (see later). Commentators such as David Harvey (1989) – who Castells does cite – have referred to this as the annihilation of space by time, or time–space compression. Instantaneous global communications flows make space shrink, arguably to nothing. Our experience of space, of distance, is profoundly mediated by time: journey time makes us feel how near or far places are, dependent on mode of transport. The world feels smaller from a jet plane than it does on foot. The same goes for communication: a letter to the USA takes days to arrive, an email the blink of an eye (or a cursor). So the space of flows has a set of temporalities, or rhythms, too: fast flows leave jetstreams, slow flows leave snail trails. And nodes can be 'sticky' too, attempting to slow down the flows that land (of course, alternatively they can be shiny, so flows bounce off).

But the space of flows isn't just this chaotic globe of frantic flows landing, bouncing and swirling overhead; while Castells says at one point that the space of flows 'connects places as nodes of networks of instrumentality' and that 'these places are not meaningful in themselves, but only as nodes of these networks' (Castells and Ince 2003: 57), where they land, how they land, and how they leave again does matter, is meaningful. But places are only places in so far as they are nodes; like workers, places can be switched off, routed round. The connection is very clear when we consider labour, in fact, given Castells' aphorism that capital is global but labour is local: the 'nodeness' of places is in part a function of the labour available there, both self-programming and generic. Flows will come if the conditions are right, but they can just as easily leave if they are wrong. As Castells (2000b: 10) succinctly puts it, 'Globalization is highly selective.' Moreover, this new geography is about the power of networks, not networks of power.

NETWORK CITIES

As noted, so-called global cities are prime nodes or hubs in the space of flows. This raises for Castells, and for us, an interesting conundrum: given the disembedding qualities of the network society, given that time-space compression 'frees' people from the constraints of geography, and given all the futurology about new ways of 'wired living', why do cities still exist? Even more than exist, in fact: the world is becoming more urbanized (see Graham 2003). Part of the answer comes back to the network logic: the network needs nodes, otherwise it would be pure flow. Castells draws on his previous work with Peter Hall on 'technopoles' (Castells and Hall 1994) as part of his explanation, noting that 'milieux of innovation' tend to be clustered around urban centres, for a number of reasons, including those management buzz words, synergy and added value. This phenomenon has attracted widespread academic and policy-making attention recently, as people have tried to unlock the magic formula that makes some cities more attractive to innovators and creatives – who are seen as the saviours of cities ravaged by the shift to post industrialism (or informationalism) that gutted urban centres across the world, and also as the engines of a new inter-urban competitivenss, as cities promote themselves to attract wealth and talent (Florida 2002).

There's also a chicken-and-egg dimension to the equation, in that innovative and creative milieux attract other innovators and creatives, other self-programmable workers. And the infrastructure that builds up to service these milieux – the consumption spaces, taste cultures and so on – are attractive, too (Jayne 2005). As Castells puts it, the global city 'tends to generate a style of architecture, a certain type of cosmopolitan aesthetics, and a series of facilities that characterize the lifestyles of the global elite' (Castells and Ince 2003: 57) – restaurants serving *sashimi*, for example, or the assorted 'VIP spaces' that offer a classy welcome. So the space of flows is a network of places that are 'connected around one common, simultaneous social practice' (ibid.: 56): not just the node of electronic communication, but also the site of a constellation of economic, social, cultural and political activities.

Castells makes a number of other insightful comments on the global city in the network society. One is that 'The global city is made of many bits and pieces of cities around the world' (Castells and Ince 2003: 57); another is that 'The global city is not a place, but a process' (Castells 1996a / 2000: 286). Part of this process is about disembedding: global cities emphasize their interconnection with other global cities, and downplay their own proximate hinterlands, leading to what Castells calls an intra-metropolitan dualism (see below). Some global cities are mono-functional, but in some senses this no longer matters as they are patched into a network that constitutes the whole. However, like previous mono-industrial cities, the dominance of a single function can render them fragile, subject to the changing flows that may bypass them to find better functionality elsewhere. Inter-urban competitiveness and intra-urban dualism are the twin features of the global network city, therefore. The space of flows impacts on urban form as well as function, Castells argues, simultaneously producing concentration and decentralization: unending urban, suburban and exurban sprawl, edge cities and megacities are variants on what he calls the informational city; these new urban forms, he adds, mean that 'the great urban paradox of the twenty-first century is that we could be living in a predominantly urban world without cities' (Castells 2005: 57) – without what we could hitherto recognize as cities, that is.

Megacities, which he later renames mega-metropolitan regions (Castells 2005), with populations in excess of 10 million, are the primary nodes of the global economy: 'concentrating the directional, productive, and managerial upper functions of all power over the planet; the control of the media; the real politics of power; and the symbolic capacity to create and diffuse messages. ... Megacities articulate the global economy, link up the informational networks, and concentrate the world's power' (Castells 1996a / 2000: 403 – 4). They are globally connected and locally disconnected, often agglomerations of cities and towns of various sizes. An exemplar is China's Pearl River Delta region, soon to be even more mega, Castells argues, as it morphs into the Hong Kong-Shenzhen-Canton-Pearl River Delta-Macau-Zhuhai metropolitan regional system, with a population well over 50 million. Embarking on futurology once more, Castells predicts that such agglomerated mega-metropolitan regions will become the most representative urban form of the twenty-first century, even though they have their own significant and growing problems, such as inadequate transport infrastructure, given that people still commute rather than telecommute (even if their commuting is electronically enhanced, through the use of laptops, BlackBerrys, mobile phones, etc.). What we are witnessing, Castells (2001b) writes, is 'the emergence of multi-modal metropolitan mobility', as nomadic workers shuttle back and forth; the individualization of working patterns, discussed earlier, only serves to heighten this, as work seeps into other parts of our lives. Networked mobility comes to characterize everyday life in the megacity: 'moving physically while keeping the networking connection to everything we do is a new realm of the human adventure, one about which we know little' (Castells 2005: 54).

DUAL CITIES

As already mentioned, a stark feature of contemporary urban form – and one predicted to become heightened in the future – is the intra-metropolitan dualism. The global city is many cities at once: Sassen (1999) writes that each global city simultaneously contains multiple cities: the corporate, the postindustrial, the third world – layered over each other, and often in conflict. Moreover, Castells highlights another key spatial dualism, between the space of flows and the space of places: 'The space of flows does not permeate down to the whole realm of human experience in the network society. Indeed, the overwhelming majority of people, in advanced and traditional societies alike, live in places, and so perceive their space as place-based' (Castells 1996a /

2000: 423). Places are localized, rooted, and people derive meaning from that rootedness. While Castells appears to romanticize place, and (in his earlier work especially) to overplay the antinomy between global and local that flows and places embody, he reiterates the crucial point that 'people do still live in places' (ibid.: 428), even if the meaning of those places is transformed by the logic of networks and flows.

In later writing and talks, Castells revises his view slightly, to see the space of flows and the space of places as more coterminous, or folded together – he even talks of '*cyborg cities*, or hybrid cities made up by the intertwining of flows and places' (Castells 2005: 54, emphasis in orginal). He also sees an error in his own prior articulation of the space of flows only to the techno-elites; because the space of flows is now predominantly about electronic communications, 'people of all kinds, wishing to do all kinds of things, can occupy this space of flows and use it for their own purposes' (Castells and Ince 2003: 58). The key example he refers to as 'grassrooting' the space of flows (Castells 1999) – the use of the network, the use of flows, by social movements, such as anti-globalization protests (Castells 2005). And in *The Internet Galaxy* (2001b), he further points to more varied uses of the space of flows to constitute a new public space, or agora, for open discussion of … well, of anything and everything. Some of this is 'political', some of it is 'progressive'. As he had argued before, the fact that some network content is far from progressive should not be used as a justification for tighter control or censorship on the net: 'The internet brings us face to face with the mirror of who we actually are. So I would rather work on ourselves than close down the net' (Castells 1999: 298).

There is another powerful urban dualism to consider in the network society: 'the simultaneous growth and decline of economies and societies within the same metropolitan area' (Castells 2002 [1996]: 132). Now, this is not simply the dualism of the space of flows and the space of places, as Castells had earlier conceived it. Things are more complex than that, and the relationships between growth and decline are still being mapped and analysed. Socioeconomic polarization between cities and within cities is the key point to remember: 'splintering urbanism' is the hallmark of the network society (Graham and Marvin 2001). Perhaps we should talk of 'glocal cities', then: at once global and local (Castells 2001b).

Indeed, in his most recent work, Castells turns his full focus to the city in the age of information, diagnosing its maladies and suggesting remedies. What is being lost in mega-urban sprawl and flow is 'the culture of cities', the role of cities as sites of cultural communication (Castells 2005). Public spaces 'as sites of spontaneous social interaction' are needed, not to encourage assimilation but to promote 'sharing the city by irreversibly distinct cultures and identities' (ibid.: 52) – a common theme in recent commentaries on the future of cities (e.g. Amin and Thrift 2002). Castells' programme for urban rejuvenation calls for a focus on communication in the broad sense:

> Restoring functional communication by metropolitan planning; providing spatial meaning by a new symbolic nodality created by innovative architectural projects; and reinstating the city in its urban form by the practice of urban design focused on the preservation, restoration, and construction of public space as the epitome of urban life.
>
> (Castells 2005: 59)

TIMELESS TIME

Space and time are closely related in the logic of networks and flows. In place of Harvey's (1989) time - space compression, where space is 'annihilated' by time, or Giddens' (1991) time - space distanciation, where the link between time and space is decoupled, Castells talks of the space of flows and timeless time. This means a number of things. First, and most obviously, it refers to speeding up. Making things faster is one of the most important imperatives of the information age (Erkisen 2001), so much so that it has birthed its own countermovement or cultural commune, in 'slow living' (Parkins and Craig 2006). So instantaneity is one form of timeless time. Another is called by Castells desequencing: as a result of living in a multimedia age with limitless access to streams of live and archived material, as well as ever more wondrous ways to predict or imagine the future, we are exposed to a montage of instants wrenched from temporal context: past, present and future are disassembled and reassembled for us and by us (see below). Without the anchoring of temporality, we live, as some postmodern commentators argue, in a 'perpetual present': the future arrives almost before we've thought of it, the past comes back at us in soundbites: 'we live ... in the encyclopedia of historical experience, all our tenses at the same time, being able to reorder them in a composite created by our own fantasy or our interests' (Castells 2002 [1996]: 131). Greater capacity for archiving our own lives, for example through digital photography, only enhances this experience, as we review and edit the masses of pasts we collect and store (Van Dijk 2005).

Outside of personal experience, timeless time is evident for Castells in split-second financial transactions on the global market, in so-called 'instant wars' comprising surgical strikes, and in the technological transformation of the lifecycle, through new reproductive technologies, anti-ageing and even, through cryogenics, the idea of deferring death. So we have a curious mix: the culture of the ephemeral and of the eternal. Castells calls this the breaking down of 'rhythmicity', and he is strikingly critical of its manifestations and motivations. He is, of course, also mindful that most people do still live by biological time and clock time; as with his discussion of the space of flows, timeless time primarily characterizes dominant social groups and functions in the network society. Yet variants are experienced outside of elites, for example in television's endless recycling of its own past, in 'retrofuturism', in the growing popularity and availability of aesthetic surgery procedures, or in the policy concept of 'work-life balance'.

SUMMARY

The space of flows is Castells' conceptualization of the geography of the network society: a global array of disjunctive flows, of different things (but increasingly of electronic things and knowledge things) that move around the world, emanating from and landing in nodes, i.e. places. Global cities are the prime movers of the space of flows, and likely to be more so as they morph into megacities or metropolitan regions, ironically the ideal urban form of the information age. But cities are riven by contradiction and duality: social polarization is getting worse. Where he used to see an opposition between the dominant space of flows and the switched-off space of places, Castells now presents a more complex picture, due in part to the 'grassrooting' of the space of flows by social movements. Time as well as space is warped by the network society, at least for dominant groups and functions. It is accelerated, randomized and desquenced, leading to timeless time and temporal perturbations that upset the former rhythms of life.

3 REAL VIRTUALITY

Real virtuality, Castells' easy pun on virtual reality, opens up a space to discuss the culture of the network society. As might be expected, this is a culture heavily shaped by the media; only the old-fashioned mass media, feeding its mass audience a standardized product, has all-but gone, replaced by the proliferating multimedia or micro-media of 'narrow-casting', the many-to-many communications of the Internet, and the flattening of distinctions between producers and consumers of media content. As we shall see, the culture of real virtuality is woven from the heterogeneous experiences of the new multimedia environment, the 'global hypertext' (Castells 2001a: 170).

MULTIMEDIA

At the heart of Castells' analysis of real virtuality is the link between communication and culture: 'culture is mediated and enacted through communication' (Castells 1996a / 2000: 328), meaning that transformations in modes of communication, including those in communications technologies, have profound implications for culture. Here is one instance of the technological determinism that critics detect in *The Information Age* (Van Dijk 1999; Webster 2002): technological change precipitates cultural change. But I think we need to set this (very valid) criticism aside for now, and sketch the main argument Castells is making.

Castells highlights the main features of new communication media, including its increasing segmentation and diversification, and its move towards greater interactivity. The days of mass media – when a standardized product was piped to audiences imagined as homogeneous – are largely over. Now media content is customized, targeted at niche markets identified through relentless market research (the use of focus groups in particular) and test screenings. Media becomes demand-led, rather than supply-led, and content providers attempt to capture particular market segments by the bespoke tailoring of their output. On-demand television, whether in terms of pay-per-view or in terms of systems that give viewers greater 'control' over programming (such as Tivo or Sky+; see O'Sullivan 2005), reconfigures the one-to-many logic of mass media to a one-to-a-select-few logic, for example.

Then, of course, there's the Internet. As a platform for media content delivery, the Internet has diversified and segmented to a dizzying degree. Adapting its horizontal networking, the Internet is argued to have flattened the distinction between producer and consumer, making all users 'prosumers'. It is argued to have further transformed the one-to-many logic, offering instead one-to-one and many-to-many at once. Castells (1996a / 2000) writes a list of personalized media devices that includes personal stereos, CMC and cable TV. The list is now inevitably out of date given the fast pace of innovation, with no mention of MP3 players or file sharing, nor of still-evolving and ever-hybridizing content streams, platforms and devices: weblogs, moblogs, podcasts, 3-G mobiles, BlackBerrys ... (though these may be antiques by the time you read this!). This proliferation only strengthens Castells' main point: 'we are not living in a global village, but in customized cottages globally produced and locally distributed' (Castells 1996a / 2000: 341). Narrowcasting has replaced broadcasting, but the sources of the narrowcasts are anywhere and everywhere, and the breadth of coverage in terms of content unimaginably wide. So multimedia culture is at once global (in reach) and local (i.e. personalized): it is *glocal*. Moreover his analysis dampens critics' claims of technological determinism, in that he is clear that new uses for media platforms and content are often unprogrammed, unexpected: new technologies are 'adapted, not just adopted' (ibid.: 363). Or, as he put it in a later discussion: 'The wonderful thing about technology is that people end up doing with it something very different from what was originally intended' (Castells 2001b: 195). While this doesn't take him down the road towards the social construction of technology (SCOT), it does show a sensitivity to producing a more complex and nuanced picture.

NARROWCASTING

In place of mass audience broadcasting, where a standardized product is distributed to a group assumed to be relatively homogeneous, narrowcasting means to send 'data' to a specific segment of recipients. Pay-TV is an example, in that channels are sent only to subscribers. So-called 'push technologies' which send information to subscribers over the Internet are another form for narrowcasting. **Podcasting** is a fast-developing method of distributing audio streams via the Internet, allowing users to subscribe to a feed of MP3s and often using automatic downloading of audio-files onto portable MP3 players or personal computers. Podcasting enables independent producers to create self-published 'radio shows', and gives broadcast radio programmes a new distribution method. Podcasting of video is currently developing. The term derives from iPod, the brand name of Apple's MP3 player (which has come to act as the generic name for MP3 players, as Hoover did earlier for vacuum cleaners). A **weblog** (or **blog**) is a web-based publication consisting primarily of periodic articles, usually marked by date and time, and often in a diary-like format. The creator is known as a blogger, undertaking some blogging. Blogs range in scope and scale as well as in form and content, and can cover every imaginable topic. Fast-growing and as yet under-researched, blogs have been a very significant form of on-line self-publishing, in some ways like more expansive and interactive personal home pages. A **moblog** is a blog containing content uploaded from portable devices such as mobile phones or BlackBerrys.

MULTIMEDIA CULTURES

If we move to explore Castells' view on how these technologies change culture by changing communication, we can isolate four important points. The first is that the newness of new media culture is contestable: 'old' pre-existing cultural forms and practices are absorbed and reworked in the network society (an example he gives is karaoke). The interactions between media, culture and society outlined in Castells' formulation of real virtuality are at times unclear about the issue of causality (Van Dijk 1999): the media is seen as 'supporting' broader social and cultural changes sometimes, but at other times it seems to be provoking change. The second point is that change is occurring, and media is part of that process. The first change, already noted, is cultural differentiation, mirrored in media segmentation – resulting in multicultural multimedia. The second change is stratification based on access to media, both in terms of time and money, and in terms of cultural capital. So some people remain passive consumers – they are, he says, 'interacted' rather than interacting; others are simply excluded from multimedia culture. This distinction between interacting and interacted echoes other critics' observations about those with the skill and resources to shape media content, and those who can still only consume it (Bell 2001).

The third point is the mixing up of different kinds of content across platforms, the blurring of forms and genres, the convergence of different formats. This is especially notable on the Internet, now that audio, still and moving images (real-time and recorded) can be sent and received by both 'professional' content producers and by 'amateurs' (another distinction fast becoming meaningless); 3-G phones and the predicted 'mobile Internet' will only intensify this blurring – or at least that's their promise. And, fourth, Castells notes that media platforms between them now 'capture within their domain most cultural expressions' (Castells 1996a: 372), meaning the end of any distinction or separation between print and audiovisual media, between high and popular culture, between education and entertainment (edutainment) and between information and advertising (infomercials). Using a search engine on the Internet is an easy illustration of many of the features Castells lists: any search turns up radically different kinds of material, from equally different sources, in multiple formats. The relentless accretion and archiving of material online, on websites, weblogs and so on means that more and more cultural content is being captured, to be recombined and reused in myriad ways: 'All culture is, in this way, eternally available, although at the same time curiously ephemeral' (McGuigan 1999: 114).

Moreover, the increasing multi-functionality of communications devices compounds this: mobile phone manufacturer Nokia (one of Castells' favourite case studies) has apparently taken to calling itself the world's biggest camera manufacturer, now that mobile phones have (still and video) cameras almost as standard. Having a camera on your phone has made everyone a potential paparazzi, with pics of celebrities a marketable commodity thanks to the tabloidization of culture (*Hello!* and *heat* magazines being cases in point). Then of course there's mobile phone ringtones, which have blurred telephony and music, first by producing ringtone versions of pop songs then, thanks to the Crazy Frog, by having hit records (not to mention posters, T-shirts, promo videos, etc.) based on ringtones. Such multidirectional cross-fertilization and hybridization present us with a complex set of interconnected ideas, sounds and images, which Castells describes as the global hypertext.

The complex convergence of multimedia sketched out above heightens this process. Taking the Internet as his main exemplar, Castells writes that we each have our own personalized hypertext, or hypermedia, carried in our minds, making connections between the many cultural communiqués we experience on a daily basis. As we become more 'media savvy', more attuned to this intertextuality, so it is more cleverly deployed by media producers – perhaps most notably makers of advertising – who exploit our enjoyment in making connections. All around us, then, myriad fragments of media texts are strung together and these, Castells ultimately argues, now constitute culture. This is, then, 'an individual hypertext

CRAZY FROG

Crazy Frog started life as 'The Annoying Thing', a short computer animation made to accompany a computer sound effect that emulates a moped engine. The Annoying Thing, a.k.a. Crazy Frog, is a strange anthropomorphic frog-like creature, who rides an invisible / imaginary moped accompanied by an odd, sing-song nonsense lyric. Tapping into the craze for novelty ringtones among mobile phone users (and the longer-running craze for novelty records), Crazy Frog was sold to mobile phone users, and then went on to be used in a succession of music releases, with accompanying promo videos, featuring Crazy Frog adding his characteristic 'A-ring-ding-ding' lyric to previous tracks. A CD single released in the UK reached the top chart position, at around the time that downloads and ringtones began to be recognized as formats for releasing music. Playing knowingly on its own annoyingness, Crazy Frog caused a media stir in the UK, and is notable for reversing or mixing-up the relationship between pop music and mobile telephony.

HYPERTEXT

The idea of hypertext has long been important to the technologies of information storage and retrieval centred on computers. It is connected to the invention of the world wide web, and has been the site of lots of experimental work and critical work. Hypertext refers to the connections between one 'text' and another (also called hyperlinks). While strictly speaking the term means embedded links connecting written texts via computer networks, the term has been broadened out, so that text here means any form of communicative content, whether a book or a painting or an opera or a soap opera – though purists might say we should really be talking about 'hypermedia' here. Texts connect or refer to other texts, either through explicit connections implanted by the text's creator, as when a film director pays homage to a predecessor by copying their signature style, or, less consciously, as the producer of a text inevitably draws on previous cultural codes, experiences and resources. Moreover, consumers of texts make connections, too, both those intended by the producer and those unintended ones that maybe they alone see. We are all of us hypertexting all of the time, making connections to help us make sense of texts; as Castells says, 'the hypertext is inside us' as our minds endlessly process culture (2001b: 202).

made of multi-modal cultural expressions recombined in new forms and new meanings' (ibid.: 203). But the connections are so dense that other people have often also made those links.

CULTURE OF REAL VIRTUALITY

The culture of virtual reality, our culture in the network society, is tagged by Castells by flipping the idea of virtual reality, which is used to describe computer-based simulations of real environments. For a while, there was an awful lot of hype about virtual reality, about how it would lead to us living out radically new experiences mediated by digital simulations (Rheingold 1991). While simulated environments have been developed in a range of contexts, their widespread diffusion has not yet occurred. Instead of virtual reality, we have real virtuality. In fact, we always have had: 'reality, as experienced, has always been virtual because it is always perceived through symbols that frame practice' (Castells 1996a / 2000: 372). While largely sidestepping the considerable debate about what 'virtual' and 'real' mean (see Shields 2002), Castells sees culture as virtual in that it is mediated, but real nonetheless:

> Reality (that is, people's material / symbolic existence) is entirely captured, fully immersed in a virtual image setting, in the world of make believe, in which appearances are not just on the screen through which experience is communicated, but they become the experience.
>
> (Castells 1996a / 2000: 373)

As Van Dijk (1999) and other critics have noted, this formulation is close to French philosopher Jean Baudrillard's notion of simulation and the hyperreal (see Lane 2000), in which simulations become decoupled from the real, and in the end come in fact to replace reality.

For Castells, the culture of real virtuality has a number of important characteristics, some of them already discussed. First, there is its inclusiveness, its comprehensive 'capture' of all cultures (although there remain problems of language, with English still dominant in cyberspace). Second, because it is part of the network society, it follows the network logic, of on or off – to be in the network is to be part of culture, to be switched off is to be excluded. Third, its diversity and multi-modality means it can accommodate cultural differences; it doesn't require us all to be the same, but offers something for everyone (with all the pros and cons that brings). This is not to say there are no barriers to participation, as already noted. In fact, ability to participate is seen by Castells as a crucial index of

JEAN BAUDRILLARD

French social theorist Jean Baudrillard (1929 –) is associated with postmodern theory and critiques of media and consumer society. He is probably best known for his formulation of the notion of hyperreality, and in particular hyperreality in the United States; for his theory of simulation and simulacra (where the 'real' is progressively replaced by the hyperreal simulacrum, more real than reality); and for his controversial pronouncements on the first Gulf War as a 'simulation' of war.

domination: who gets to talk, who to listen, and who is kept out of the loop? Fourth, the new media culture weakens traditional transmissions if they are still sent through other means (religion must become real-virtual, he argues, if it is to retain any place in this culture). And fifth, the culture of real virtuality radically reconfigures relations of space and time, creating or at least propagating the space of flows and timeless time.

Interestingly, in tracking the genealogy of this idea, we can see how in 'The net and the self', Castells (1996b) saw a potential threat in real virtuality: 'The social consequence of such technological developments is the growing tension between globalization and individualization in the audio-visual universe, bringing about the danger of the breakdown of the patterns of social communication between world information flows and the pulse of personal experiences' (Castells 1996b: 20); in the decade since he wrote this, so much has changed in the multimedia landscape that such an opposition has become nonsense: global information flows are full of the pulse of personal experiences, and getting ever fuller. Here is a clear example of the space of flows being grassrooted, not only in the service of social movements, but as a stage for the production and consumption – maybe better to say the 'prosumption' – of kaleidoscopic personalized hypertexts that need serve no bigger purpose than being there: 'the virtuality of this text is in fact a fundamental dimension of reality, providing the symbols and icons from which we think and thus exist' (Castells 2000b: 13). Importantly, I don't think this means the subsumption of the real by the virtual, as some critics suggest (e.g. Van Dijk 1999); it's more to do with co-existence, or maybe we might say the *convergence* of the real and the virtual.

INTERNET CULTURE

In *The Internet Galaxy*, Castells approaches the question of culture in the network society somewhat differently, by refocusing explicitly on the cultures of the Internet. This enables him to limit his analysis by switching off from scrutiny any other dimensions of the network society. Moreover, he switches off those who are only consumers or users of the Internet by arguing upfront that 'the Internet culture is the culture of the creators of the Internet' (Castells 2001b: 36). Having cleared away all other distractions, he is able to detect a four-layer structure which articulates to form this culture: the techno-meritocratic culture, the hacker culture, the virtual communitarian culture, and the entrepreneurial culture. The techno-elite we have already met, the 'no-collar' workers who provide much of the infrastructure of the Internet (software, protocols, etc.). This culture is meritocratic in that status comes from expertise, from what Donna Haraway (1991) calls 'machine skill'. Importantly, in order to have expertise recognized and thus accrue status, the culture is marked by an openness, a willingness to share ideas and outputs. This openness, Castells argues, is a product of the twin origins of the Internet, academia and hacking. This openness is also under recurrent threat as corporations colonize the Internet, the most obvious case being Microsoft's protection of its own source code (versus the open-source movement).

To discuss hacking, Castells draws heavily on the work of Pekka Himanen (2001). Dispelling the myths of hacking as deviant or criminal activity, Himanen shows the vital importance of hacking in shaping Internet culture (see also Ross 2000). Hackers also value openness and

OPEN-SOURCE

The practice of making available the source code of computer software, so that users and other developers can study, change and improve its design. Software developers may publish their software as open-source so that anybody else can explore how it works, make improvements, or develop new versions of the software. Users can input modifications that improve the performance of the program, which can then be shared by everyone using it. **Source code** contains the key information needed to understand the design of the software. Linux, initially written as a hobby by Finnish student Linus Torvalds, is one of the best known examples: unlike so-called proprietary software such as Microsoft Windows or Macintosh operating systems, which are kept 'secret', all of the source code for Linux is available to the public, over the Internet, so anyone with the requisite skill level can freely use, modify and redistribute it. Open-source has become a powerful symbol of the idea of 'information freeness' underpinning hacking culture and the Internet.

the 'spirit of informationalism' captured in the hacker slogan 'Information wants to be free'. The generally libertarian ideology of the hacking culture, which Castells arguably romanticizes, exhibits for him 'a shared belief in the power of computer networking, and a determination to keep this technological power as a common good – at least for the community of hackers' (Castells 2001b: 52). Virtual communitarians build new social networks in cyberspace, and Castells wisely sidesteps the long-running debate about whether these networks can properly be called communities or not (see Bell 2001). Importantly, he describes what participants are doing in these communities as 'self-directed networking', noting the flourishing of 'self-publishing, self-organizing, and self-networking [that] permeates the Internet' (Castells 2001b: 54) and that also connects the Internet to the social realm (rather than splitting it into off- and online worlds). In this age of moblogs and podcasts, such activities are flourishing even more.

Castells' fourth layer is Internet entrepreneurs. This group capitalized in various ways on the business opportunities they foresaw in using the Internet to make money, famously in so-called dot.com enterprises. Comprising inventors, technologists and venture capitalists, and marked by a culture of workaholism and 'superfluous consumption', this group has important similarities to and differences from the techno-meritocratic elite. Its work culture is similarly informal, but its prime motive is making money rather than displaying machine skill. People in this group are, says Castells bluntly, 'artists and prophets and greedy' (ibid.: 60); they could never have thought of or built the Internet, but now it's there they are exploiting it to the max.

SUMMARY

If informationalism is the economic manifestation of the information age, and the network society its social morphology, then real virtuality is its culture. Culture is all about communication, so radical transformations in communications technologies augur cultural change. Castells uses the term multimedia as a shorthand for the proliferating devices and forms of content available to segmented markets of 'prosumers'. Instead of mass media and mass audiences, the new media products emphasize interactivity and personalization, and the process of decoding cultural texts produces each person's own hypertext, through which they make sense of the world and their place within it. As it always is, culture is virtual (i.e. mediated by symbols) and real (i.e. it is our reality, our experience). As Castells says, his main purpose in discussing real virtuality 'is to reintegrate virtuality as core to our reality and to our experience. ... So we cannot oppose what is real and what is virtual because the virtual is a fundamental part of the real' (Castells with Catterall 2001: 20, 19).

AFTER CASTELLS

As commentators have repeatedly said – even those with criticism as their main aim – there can be no doubting that Manuel Castells has produced one of the most comprehensive, well-exemplified, sophisticated accounts of the world we live in today. And *The Information Age* trilogy is part of a lifetime's work – work that goes on as Castells revisits and road-tests his thesis. The impact and influence of his work, his research and his teaching, resonates across the social sciences, and indeed beyond (including beyond academia, for example in informing communications policy in Catalunya). While, as I said at the start of my discussion, he would probably not recognize himself by the label cyberculture theorist, his ideas and insights have nonetheless been centrally concerned with theorizing (albeit with hesitation at times) something akin to (but also more than) cyberculture. In a transdisciplinary field, and one too often wrongly associated with technophilic hype and technophobic doom, his evidence-based discussions of the economy, culture and society of the networked information age deserve esteemed recognition. Certainly he is centrally placed in what we might call an 'empirical turn' in cyberculture studies, also evident in the work of scholars publishing in the series he edits (Benner 2002; Servon 2002; Wellman and Haythornwaite 2002; Zoon 2004). Such a turn has been widely welcomed, not least for lending legitimacy to the field in these anxious academic times.

That is not to say there aren't flaws in his thesis, as critics have high-lighted, and Castells has often been only too pleased to concede – as in his reconsideration of cultural social movements in his discussion of 'grassrooting' in the space of flows, or in his more open discussion of ideas in published interviews (Castells with Catterall 2001; Castells and Ince 2003). But from this we can see the 'liveliness' of his thinking, his willingness to take on new ideas, to revise and rethink.

One aspect of the network society or information age that Castells hints at, and that he sees as of growing importance, is biotechnology, specifically genomics and genetic engineering as well as hybrid fields such as nanoscience. Seeing genetics and genomics as also about information processing and manipulation, he foresees greater commingling of compu-tational and biogenetic information networks, though he admits it may still be too early to get a handle on these newer developments (Ince 2004 [2000]). Relatedly, he has shown a growing interest in issues of intellec-tual property rights and in the open-source movement (see, for example, Castells 2001b). So, in one sense, what comes after Castells is … more Castells. Given his prodigious productivity, there will certainly be more work forthcoming, as he pursues these and other intellectual interests (see Roberts 2004 [1999]).

NEWNESS

Earlier in my discussion, I noted that critics have often queried what exactly is new about the world as it is today, or Castells' way of under-standing it (e.g. Webster 2002). Castells himself sidestepped this criticism by saying off-hand that the question of newness is *boring* (Castells and Ince 2003): he's right and wrong, I think. Right not to let the question of new-ness snag or stall his analyses, but wrong in being perhaps too dismissive. To be sure, it doesn't matter to anyone but a few academics whether there has been a revolution or a paradigm shift. And getting a measure on the relative 'weight' of change and continuity seems impossible, and cer-tain to end only in further disagreement. Castells' project is political as well as intellectual; he keeps reminding us that changing the way the world is starts by understanding how it got to be that way. Perhaps this also means asking what's at stake in the question of newness, asking why it is something that people get fixated by. Certainly newness is a powerful lubricant, in all kinds of ways, for the network society.

The turn in the trajectory of Castells' work mentioned a moment ago, in relation to grassrooting, reveals more than the author's willingness to change his mind. It reminds us, too, that newness is an inevitable feature of the network society, not only as new technologies are invented and marketed, but also as people find new, unexpected uses for technologies. These can be progressive or regressive, as Castells is well aware of from his studies of social movement networking. So Jan Van Dijk (1999: 128) is right to say that Castells' trilogy is 'time-sensitive': the pace of change, both in terms of innovation and in terms of creative appropriation, haunts all of us who write about new technologies. But that shouldn't stop us from researching and writing about the world around us, trying to understand it. (I for one wonder if anyone will remember the Crazy Frog by the time this book is actually read! – itself a sign of the non-newness of writing books in the age of information flows.)

Ultimately, then, Castells has provided us with a very useful analysis of the information age (or whatever you choose to name it). True, it is imperfect in parts, and has been subject to extensive criticism, leading to revision. Theory can't stand still in the fast-moving network society, and the sheer complexity and changeability of the world today almost inevitably works against any attempt to produce a grand narrative that can sum it all up. But we need to read and think about Castells, agree and disagree with him, keep reviewing and revising, supplementing and retooling, this elaborate, rich and multifaceted study. As Frank Webster (2002: 123) concludes: 'No analyst of information nowadays can fail to start with the work on Manuel Castells. But nor can an adequate account stop with *The Information Age*' – a point I am more than sure that Manuel Castells would be in agreement with.

WHY HARAWAY?

Understanding the world is about living inside stories.

(Haraway with Goodeve 2000: 107)

First of all, for her 'Cyborg Manifesto', first published in 1985, revised and collected into her book *Simians, Cyborgs, and Women* in 1991, and relentlessly anthologized since then. This essay has become, as Constance Penley and Andrew Ross (1991: 1) put it, a 'cult text' – hugely influential in cyberculture studies, and way beyond; as her former student Zoë Sofoulis (2002: 84) rightly says, the Cyborg Manifesto generated an enormous 'cyberquake' reverberating across intellectual domains, setting out 'multidisciplinary questions, connections, and directions for further research'; as she adds, its 'rumbles in the field of cyberstudies, a field it helped to initiate, are still being felt at the beginning of the 21st century'. In the magazine *Wired*, Hari Kunzru (1998: 1) goes ever further, writing that 'To boho twentysomethings, her name has the kind of cachet usually reserved for techno acts or phenethylamines'. While her figuration of the cyborg has overshadowed her many other interventions to a range of important debates – an overshadowing I am inevitably also contributing to here – the ongoing aftershocks of the Manifesto make it truly one of the *ur*-texts of cyberculture theory.

But Haraway is about so much more than that. In interviews, when pressed to summarize the overarching concerns of her work, she describes it using variants of the question: 'what counts as nature [or culture] in the world today?' or 'what's at stake in what counts ... ?'. She asks a lot – what's at stake in things, who benefits, and how might the stakes be changed? – for her work is motivated by a deep politics, though her harshest critics wrongly see her as a postmodernist prankster. She is not; as I hope to be able to show you. Haraway's work takes seriously the stories in which we live, and she also wants to find ways to tell better ones, to *live* better ones; what Joseph Schneider (2005: 162) poetically calls 'imagining and writing elsewheres'. Her key methods – diffraction, figuration, situated knowledges – are all about this, as we shall see. So, in one sense Haraway doesn't really 'fit in' here, in this strange coterie of cybertheorists; I'm sure she'd be both amused and bemused at being included. But her work is simply too important to ignore; the sin of omission would be greater than that of uneasy inclusion.

First let's take a brief look at her life, before moving on to examine the life, or more accurately lives, of her cyborg. Donna Haraway was born in Denver, Colorado, USA, in 1944. She has talked extensively about her life and work in a number of published interviews – Haraway, it must be said, 'gives good interview' – and the Further Reading section points up the most useful and interesting of these conversations, or what Schneider (2005: 6) names 'the stories of her selves that she tells'. Her upbringing was Catholic and, while she says she has become anti-Catholic, she nevertheless acknowledges the religion's imprint on her way of thinking. After high school she went on to attend Colorado College, taking an unusual triple major – but entirely in keeping with the trajectory of her intellectual development – in English literature, philosophy and zoology. After graduating she spent a year in Paris, before enrolling for a PhD in biology at Yale University, 'made possible', she observed, 'by Sputnik's impact on U.S. science-education policy', thus implicating her squarely in technoculture (Haraway 1991: 173). During her studies she progressively turned towards the history of biology, and completed a thesis on the use of organic metaphors in biology, tracking different ways of thinking within scientific practice. The thesis would later become *Crystals, Fabrics, and Fields: Metaphors of Organicism in Twentieth-century Developmental Biology* (1976/2004). With her then partner, she moved for a short time to the University of Hawaii in Honolulu, before taking a post at Johns Hopkins

University in the Department of the History of Science. From here she started research on primatology, published in book form as *Primate Visions: Gender, Race, and Nature in the World of Modern Science* (1989), a book she would later see as the first volume in a trilogy with shared concerns about Western science, society, nature and culture. In 1980 she was appointed to an interdisciplinary unit at the University of California at Santa Cruz (UCSC), the Board in the History of Consciousness, where she remains in post today, and from where she researched and wrote a number of landmark essays; publications that are, as Schneider (2005: 12) sums up, 'both pathbreaking and pathmaking' (Schneider provides a very clear summary of her life and work; see also Clough and Schneider 2001 and the book-length interview, *How Like a Leaf*, by Haraway with Goodeve 2000).

Along with a string of highly influential papers, Haraway completed her trilogy of interconnected books, first with *Simians, Cyborgs, and Women* (1991) and then with her book with a complex and punny title, formed as an email address and summoning another series of particular figures, or what she names 'material-semiotic entities': *Modest_Witness@Second_Millennium.FemaleMan©_Meets_OncoMouse*™ (1997), arguably her most challenging and important work. More recently, her attention has shifted towards relationships, or better relationalities, between dogs and humans, rewriting the Manifesto format to think through the idea of 'companion species' (Haraway 2003a) as the start of what she sees as a continuation of her work on 'naturecultures' and on the menagerie or 'kinship of feminist figurations' (Haraway 2004a).

NATURECULTURES

Haraway uses this neologism to emphasize the impossibility of separating the natural and the cultural – what we think of as 'nature' is 'one of culture's most startling and non-innocent products' (Haraway 1991/1988a: 109). But culture is also the product of nature, in that humans are a biological species. In her work on 'companion species', for example, Haraway talks of the naturecultures of the co-evolution of dogs and humans. Separating nature and culture is an ideological act, so the questions turn to 'What's at stake in naming some things as nature and others as culture?' and 'Who benefits?'

Surveying her own work when assembling a *Reader*, Haraway comments that 'I feel that I have written the same paper twenty times' (2004a: 2), seeing the connections that draw her to particular ideas and ways of thinking – later she concludes that 'Perhaps the same paper needs to be written again and again' (ibid.: 5) in the hope of building what she calls 'more livable worlds'. She sees gathered in her work 'my queer family of feminists, anti-racists, scientists, scholars, genetically engineered lab rodents, cyborgs, dogs, dog people, vampires, modest witnesses, writers, molecules, and both living and stuffed apes' (ibid.: 3), a kin group that captures her call, in *Modest_Witness*, for 'models of solidarity and human unity and difference rooted in friendship, work, partially shared purposes, intractable collective pain, inescapable mortality, and persistent hope' (Haraway 1997: 265).

So, as it should be becoming clear by now, Haraway is about much more than the cyborg, though she is arguably best known for that queer kin. Trying to sum up her work, Schneider (2005: 21) writes that 'she hopes to encourage a way of seeing, thinking, and acting together that begins to change the way humans and the many others to whom they are connected know and live together now and in the future' – reminding us once more of the ethical and political heart of Haraway's writing. A final comment from Schneider with his coauthor Patricia Ticineto Clough, in an earlier summary of Haraway's life and work, seems a fitting place to end this introduction, reinforcing the politics at stake here, before we focus in on the cyborg:

> No other cultural critic has had more influence than Haraway in bringing forward difficult questions that point to the ways scientific work and knowledge are interimplicated with a wide range of global and local practices of exploitation and domination. In this work she has established links between cultural studies and science studies that benefit both lines of work.
>
> (Clough and Schneider 2001: 345)

HARAWAY'S
KEY IDEAS

1 CYBORG

I feel it is necessary to give Haraway's cyborg a lengthy treatment here; it has had a long and complex life, or series of lives, and the 'cyberquake' it generated rumbles on in endless aftershocks. So I shall start with the Cyborg Manifesto, *not* the birthplace of the cyborg, not its 'origin story' – these things being resolutely un-cyborgian – but as the place where the author began to think through a particular and located figuration, in a particular intellectual and political context, which needs to be mapped out with some precision if we are going to understand the significance (and also the limitations) of thinking with the cyborg. And like its sci-fi kin the replicants, in the movie *Blade Runner* (1982), the cyborg has been tasked with a lot of difficult and dirty work, so we also need to spend quite a bit of time exploring that here.

CYBORG MANIFESTO

> You can tell you are in the presence of a cyborg figure when you feel a new world coming into being around you.
>
> (Myerson 2000: 24)

In a critical overview of Haraway's work, Rene Munnik (2001) describes the 'short prehistory' of the Cyborg Manifesto: in 1983 Haraway contributed two papers to a conference, 'New Machines, New Bodies, New Communities: Political Dilemmas of a Cyborg Feminist' and 'The Scholar and the Feminist X: The Question of Technology', and in the following year she published a version of the Manifesto in a German journal, though that essay focused more on genetic engineering. In 1985, following a request from the editors of the journal *Socialist Review* to submit a short commentary on the state of socialist feminism in the Reagan 'Star Wars' era, the article was published therein as 'A Manifesto for Cyborgs: Science, Technology, and Socialist Feminism in the 1980s' (Haraway 1985).

Haraway describes the commissioning of the Manifesto in an interview:

> Socialist feminism had disappeared as a living social movement in the United States. Although it hardly ever existed as a living social movement in the United States, or frankly too little, it had been a kind of compelling vision, a kind of consensual hallucination anyway ... [*Socialist Review*] sent a bunch of us letters and said, 'Look, you were all socialist feminists. What happened? What does it mean in the Reagan years?' 'A Manifesto for Cyborgs' emerged as a kind of dream-space piece.
>
> (Gordon 1994: 243)

The essay was, she puts it, written 'to try to think through how to do critique, remember war and its offspring, keep ecofeminism and technoscience joined in the flesh, and generally honor possibilities that escape unkind origins' (Haraway 2004a: 3). The Manifesto was then revised and collected into *Simians, Cyborgs, and Women* along with nine other important essays on what she would later call 'naturecultures' (Haraway 1991), with the slight but important changes to its title, 'A Cyborg Manifesto: Science,

STAR WARS

Known officially as the Strategic Defence Initiative (SDI), the 'Star Wars' programme was conceived in the early 1980s, during the Reagan administration, as a space-based defence 'shield' to protect the USA from nuclear missile attack. It centred on the development of a satellite-mounted x-ray laser curtain, and the programme was dubbed 'Star Wars' by critics who saw it as little more than science fiction. The programme was abandoned a decade after its inception.

Technology, and Socialist-Feminism in the Late Twentieth Century'. It has been lively in print ever since, tinkered with by Haraway and by others, reappearing in Haraway's subsequent work, as well as starring in countless *Readers* and being cited and worked over in a dizzying range of contexts (as we shall see). One last fact about the Manifesto's birth that has become almost legendary: it was the first article that Haraway wrote on a computer, her first foray into cyborg writing (Kunzru 1998). As Sofoulis (2002) writes, the Manifesto was *zeitgeisty* for lots of reasons, not least that its publication occurred at precisely the time when lots of humanities academics were starting to experience computers in their working lives, were starting to feel a bit like cyborgs themselves.

Schneider (2005: 58) quite rightly calls the Manifesto 'challenging, difficult, and exhilirating', but I think he is wrong to call it 'somewhat dated'; perhaps we should say instead that, as Haraway herself has pointed out, it belongs to a particular time and place, as noted in the story of its sourcing: it is a Reagan-era product reflecting on post-Second World War America, on technoscience and politics, or perhaps on technoscience *as* politics and vice versa. John Christie (1992: 175) also writes that the Manifesto has 'a recognizably eighties feminist political and aesthetic sensibility', that it is a kind of time capsule or period piece, even as it has lived on, endlessly cited and quoted. True, it talks of Star Wars and Reaganism, and doesn't foresee the many technoscientific challenges and adventures ahead, but its resonant shockwaves justify its longevity as much more than a relic or curio (see also Crewe 1997). But, while the cyborg has been wrenched from its historical and geographical locations, pushed back to the future and forward

SOCIALIST FEMINISM

Also known as materialist feminism, this branch of feminist theory and politics has its roots in Marxism, and argues that liberation for women can be achieved only by working to end the causes of women's oppression, which are economic and cultural. Socialist feminism thus broadens strictly Marxist feminism's focus on the central role of capitalism in the oppression of women, adding in elements from radical feminism's theorizations of patriarchy, thereby highlighting the interrelations of class and gender.

TECHNOSCIENCE

A concept widely used in interdisciplinary science and technology studies to designate the social and technological context of science. It is used to acknowledge that science and technology are inseparable, and that both are also inseparably social. Haraway (1997: 50) calls it a 'condensed signifier which mimes the implosion of science and technology' and which as such 'designates dense nodes of human and non-human actors that are brought into alliance by the material, social, and semiotic technologies through which what will count as nature and as matters of fact will get consitituted'.

to the past, it is important to see the situatedness of the cyborg, and of the Manifesto, before attending to its subsequent disembedding, stretching and morphing.

CYBORG STORYING

I want to begin by describing the Manifesto, its form and content, and then to move closer and explore its key ideas. It may be challenging and difficult, but it is definitely also exhilarating, and rewards repeat reading. The first time I attempted the Manifesto, it really made my head hurt; it still does, at times, but there's such a thrill to reading it, so many clever and funny moments, so much work. As I hold a densely annotated copy in my hand – one of several, all bearing the marks of past readings – I still keep seeing new things, new connections, new diffractions. A dreamspace piece indeed. The Manifesto comprises six interlocked sections, and I want to sketch these here.

AN IRONIC DREAM OF A COMMON LANGUAGE FOR WOMEN IN THE INTEGRATED CIRCUIT

This opening section introduces Haraway's way of thinking the cyborg and the Manifesto; the former is 'a creature of social reality as well as a creature of fiction', the latter 'an ironic political myth faithful to feminism, socialism, and materialism', to which she adds that it is 'faithful as blasphemy is faithful', starting the playful (yet deadly serious) unpicking and unpacking, redescribing and diffracting that characterizes the article (Haraway 1991: 149). Sofoulis (2002) notes that this is the most-quoted section of the Manifesto, full of telling phrases that we do indeed find littered across countless subsequent cyborg stories, though they are often pared down to aphorisms. These are among my favourites:

- By the late twentieth century, our time, a mythic time, we are all chimeras, theorized and fabricated hybrids of machine and organism; in short, we are all cyborgs. The cyborg is our ontology; it gives us our politics.

- This essay is an argument for *pleasure* in the confusion of boundaries and for *responsibility* in their construction.

- The cyborg is a creature in a post-gender worlds; it has no truck with bisexuality, pre-Oedipal symbiosis, unalienated labor, or other seductions to organic wholeness ...

- The cyborg is resolutely committed to partiality, irony, intimacy, and perversity. It is oppositional, utopian, and completely without innocence.

- Cyborgs are not reverent; they do not remember the cosmos. They are wary of holism, but needy for connection ...

- The main trouble with cyborgs ... is that they are the illegitimate offspring of militarism, patriarchal capitalism, not to mention state socialism. But illegitimate offspring are often exceedingly unfaithful to their origins. Their fathers, after all, are inessential.

(Haraway 1991: 150 – 1)

These fragments, even decoupled from their overall flow, contain so many of the key themes of the Manifesto it isn't surprising they have been copied and used in many subsequent discussions: the refusal of transcendent wholeness, the illegitimacy, the anti-psychoanalytic view, the *irony*. ... In fact, the irony of the Manifesto has been quite a source of trouble in its afterlife, being either used to dismiss the article as pointless postmodern relativism or being missed in readings that take things too literally; as Haraway says in an interview, the Manifesto was written with a 'kind of contained ironic fury', but 'the reading practices ... took me aback from the very beginning, and I learned that irony is a dangerous

CLYNES' AND KLINE'S CYBORG

Two scientists, Manfred Clynes and Nathan Kline, are credited with creating the first cyborg, or cybernetic organism, as part of their research at Rockland State Hospital, New York, into adapting the human body for space travel. As part of this work they fitted a 220g white laboratory rat with a 'Rose' osmotic pump, designed to automatically inject chemicals into the rat to control aspects of its biochemistry. In their famous 1960 paper for *Astronautics*, they not only published the now-famous photo of this cyborg, but also discussed the many modifications to human bodies necessary for a future life in space, drawing heavily on cybernetic theory; the cyborg, for Clynes and Kline, is a 'self-regulating man machine system'.

rhetorical strategy' (Markussen, Olesen and Lykke 2003: 50). So, the irony is also fury, irony used as a way to contain fury, to make it more productive. These are not the 'ramblings of a blissed-out, technobunny, fembot' (Haraway 2004a: 3); the commitment to socialist feminism, but also the critique of it (and of other feminisms), for one thing, often get stepped over by readings that wrench a few key phrases out of the article and spin their own theories from there. As I have done above; let me rectify that now.

The key component of the first section of the Manifesto is the observation of the breaching of boundaries by the cyborg, or the idea of the cyborg, that is the cybernetic organism, a fusing of the organic and the technological. As she later found out, thanks to a student, the first documented cyborg was a lab rat fitted with an osmotic pump, created by scientists interested in preparing the human body for space flight (Clynes and Kline 1995 [1960]; Haraway 1995). The space race is intertwined, of course, with the Cold War, with militarism and supremicism, making it, as Kunzru (1998: 6) says, 'a kind of scientific and military daydream'. But, Haraway argues, the cyborg is illegitimate, unfaithful, wily: it does not play by its father's rules, and can be put to different dreamwork. Thought differently, the cyborg can challenge the places from whence it came; this is part of its irony.

So part of the cyborg's challenge is that its existence – including its existence in science fiction as well as social reality – threatens fundamental boundaries that have long structured ways of understanding the world. These boundaries include those between:

- human and animal
- organism and machine
- physical and non-physical

Now, a big part of the irony is that science, or perhaps more accurately technoscience, has been at the heart of this undoing, this blurring and breaching of boundaries. To take some recent exemplars: xenotransplantation, the use of animal organs in human transplants, or sociobiology, which 'explains' human behaviour by looking at animals; smart machines (including smart weapons) that can 'think' for us and that are 'disturbingly lively' (Haraway 1991: 152); nanoscience and quantum theory, where material and immaterial are much closer together than we may have thought, where matter is energy – or, as Haraway poetically put it, where 'our best machines are made of sunshine' (ibid.: 153). In these and other ways, technoscience is troubling boundaries that have worked for so long to keep everything in its place. These tidy dualisms, integral to the Western worldview, have been ruptured as the modern technoscientific age has progressed (see also Latour 1993). For its role(s) in these 'transgressed boundaries, potent fusions and dangerous possibilities' (Haraway 1991: 154), the cyborg deserves our careful attention, our ironic handling.

But there's that bigger layer of irony to attend to: the cyborg is also implicated in 'the final imposition of a grid of control on the planet, [it is] about the final abstraction embodied in a Star Wars apocalypse waged in the name of defense, about the final appropriation of women's bodies in a masculinist orgy of war' (ibid.: 154). That's one way of reading the cyborg, but for Haraway that is fatalistic and fatal: better to at least try to build more livable worlds with this cyborg, better to think it and us differently:

> From another perspective, a cyborg world might be about lived social and bodily realities in which people are not afraid of their joint kinship with animals and machines, not afraid of permanently partial identities and contradictory standpoints. The political struggle is to see from both perspectives at once because each reveals both dominations and possibilities unimaginable from the other vantage point. ... Cyborg unities are monstrous and illegitimate; in our

> present political circumstances, we could hardly hope for more potent myths for
> resistance and recoupling.
>
> (Haraway 1991: 154)

Absolutely not a technobunny's blissed-out ramblings, then: a Manifesto
in the truest sense, a call to action, to change (see also Bartsch, DiPalma
and Sells 2001).

FRACTURED IDENTITIES

In the second main section of the Manifesto, Haraway situates her work
'in relation to issues within feminist theory, including questions of identities in multi-ethnic communities where essentialisms don't seem to work,
at a time when the category "woman" has lost its "innocence" as a political, analytic, and epistemological starting point' (Sofoulis 2002: 85). So
this section concerns feminism in the 1980s, the splintering of feminist
theory and politics into multiple feminisms – a fracturing too of the idea
of a universal or essential category of 'woman' and of 'women's experience',
destabilized by the vectors of difference (Weedon 1999). A time of heated
debate within feminism, then, out of which Haraway hopes to salvage
something, a new way of talking about identity, about feminism, about
domination and resistance: 'What kind of politics could embrace partial,
contradictory, permanently unclosed constructions of personal and collective selves and be faithful, effective – and, ironically, socialist feminist?',
she tellingly asks (Haraway 1991: 157). Can feminism still being a meaningful politics, an identification, once difference is fully acknowledged?

In 'Fractured Identities', Haraway works through some ways of
addressing this issue, starting with ways she finds unsatisfactory, critiquing both socialist and radical feminism, while wanting to hold on to
something that each offers. She rejects attempts to totalize identity or
experience, to claim to 'speak for' others under the common name
'Woman'. Yet she is also critical of the then-modish response to this,
so-called difference feminism (or postmodern feminism), preferring
instead to borrow some terms from another of her students, Chela
Sandoval: oppositional or differential consciousness, and the methodology
of the oppressed, used by Sandoval to talk about 'women of color' as a
postmodern political identification that refuses unity (but also relativism;

see Sandoval 1995). Like oppositional consciousness, then, Haraway calls for a cyborg feminism, a feminism built from 'partial [but] real connection' (Haraway 1991: 161) – a theme she develops in the next section of the Manifesto.

THE INFORMATICS OF DOMINATION

Here Haraway attempts to map out the world today, or at least a series of changes in 'worldwide social relations tied to science and technology' (Haraway 1991: 161); she produces a long chart of paired terms, comparing key terms from modernity to those of contemporary technoscience and arguing, in a way at once similar and different to Manuel Castells' informationalism, for recognizing that we are now in 'an emerging system of world order analogous in its novelty and scope to that created by industrial capitalism'; a world order built of 'scary new networks' – the informatics of domination.

Rather than repeat the whole list here – it has been reproduced by countless others – I will pick 'n' mix some pairs, and use them to illustrate the overarching lesson of the listing. First off, again echoing Castells and others, such as Jean Baudrillard, we have 'representation' replaced by 'simulation' – where the former maintains an anchor in the 'real' and the latter has come to stand in for reality. 'Scientific management in home / factory' is superseded by 'global factory / electronic cottage', 'labor' by 'robotics', 'functional specialization' with 'modular construction' – all

MICHEL FOUCAULT

Professor of the History of Systems of Thought at the College de France, Michel Foucault (1926 – 84) wrote widely and critically on social insitutions such as the prison and the mental asylum, and was concerned with how knowledge is used to produce order, to produce people as subjects, and to designate the 'normal' and the 'deviant' – to order subjects. He also developed theories of power / knowledge – the relationship between knowledge and power in modern societies, for example through surveillance; of the potentially 'productive' force of power, and of the role of discourse, or expert knowledges, in shaping societies in modernity. His work has been immensely influential across the humanities and social sciences.

similarly resonant echoes of the network society. And remember how Castells talked about the feminization of work, with the organization man replaced by the flexible woman? Haraway has a consonant pair here, too: 'family / market / factory' transposes to 'women in the integrated circuit' (see below). Lastly, at the foot of the table, we have the crunch: 'white capitalist patriarchy' becomes the 'informatics of domination'. The new world order brings new dominations; the question will inevitably turn to new resistances before the Manifesto ends, the twinning of power and resistance revealing the influence of Michel Foucault on Haraway (Sofoulis 2002).

The twin columns of the chart accomplish more than description, of course: the terms are unsettled or denaturalized by being paired, Haraway writes, the second term deconstructing (though she doesn't use that word) the first, undermining its authority as an original Truth. Or, as Jonathan Crewe (1997: 895) puts it, the chart performs an act of 'transcoding', with 'each term in the right-hand column transcoding and historically displacing its counterpart in the left-hand column'. Moreover, these new times, emblematized by the 'new' second terms, call for a new politics. For feminist theory and politics, this means attending to the informatics of domination: the actual situation of women is their integration / exploitation into a world system of production / reproduction and communication. This means addressing the new terms, not still kicking against the old ones. Hence one key route for 'reconstructing [note: *not* abandoning] socialist-feminist politics is through theory and practice addressed to the social relations of science and technology, including crucially the systems of myth and meanings structuring our imaginations' (Haraway 1991: 163). Communications sciences and biotechnologies turn the world into code – machine code, genetic code – producing 'fresh sources of power' that have to be met with 'fresh sources of analysis and political action', again showing her Foucauldianism. Understanding this is, for Haraway, crucial to the reconstruction of feminism in the times of the cyborg.

THE 'HOMEWORK ECONOMY' OUTSIDE 'THE HOME'

The new division of labour ushered in by the information age is the focus of this next short section – especially the new global working class, made up in large part of Castells' flexible women. Haraway borrows the term 'homework economy' to describe new work patterns, a 'world capitalist organizational structure ... made possible by (not caused by) the new technologies' (Haraway 1991: 166) – underemployment, casualization, insecurity, lack of welfare, and a bi-modal social structure, switched on or switched off, valued or discarded. And not just work; private life, leisure time, intimacy are all restructured by science and technology. The question for Haraway then turns towards feminist science, towards the possibilities of doing science with an oppositional consciousness, of forging a new politics of science.

WOMEN IN THE INTEGRATED CIRCUIT

Here Haraway builds on the insights of the previous section to think through 'the complexities of international gendered and ethnic divisions of labor in the globalized economy' (Sofoulis 2002: 85), using the idea and ideology of the network as 'both a feminist practice and a multinational corporate strategy' (Haraway 1991: 170), akin to Castells' grassrooting the space of flows. In fact, in this section Haraway considers a sequence of idealized capitalist spaces – home, market, workplace, state, school, hospital, church – and then riffs the (ambivalent) impacts of science and technology on each, for example:

> *Home:* Women-headed households, serial monogamy, flight of men, old women alone, technology of domestic work, paid homework, re-emergence of home sweat-shops, home-based businesses and telecommuting, electronic cottage, urban homelessness, migration, module architecture, reinforced (simulated) nuclear family, intense domestic violence.
>
> *Church:* Electronic fundamentalist 'super-saver' preachers solemnizing the union of electronic capital and automated fetish goods; intensified importance of churches in resisting the militarized state; central struggle over women's meanings and authority in religion; continued relevance of spirituality, intertwined with sex and health, in political struggle.
>
> (Haraway 1991: 171 – 2)

Interestingly, in the 2004 reprint of this article in *The Haraway Reader*, much of this section, including these lists, has been cut by the author, perhaps a reflection of the even more ambivalent outcomes of twenty more years of the informatics of domination. Out of this discussion, she moves towards a position of hope, or at least grounds for hope, in a new partial feminist politics that rejects 'the feminist dream of a common language' (Haraway 1991: 173) and does not need to resolve contradictions and find universality.

CYBORGS: A MYTH OF POLITICAL IDENTITY

Hence a return to the cyborg, this time as it has been imagined in feminist science fiction, a source which Haraway finds inspiring for its abilities to think otherwise. Calling her chosen authors 'theorists for cyborgs' (Haraway 1991), she brings all the threads together, though together in the form of a cat's cradle – a favourite metaphor of hers – rather than anything tidied up and finished. As well as science fiction, she discusses writing by 'women of color' as producing other potent fusions and boundary transgressions, as a form of cyborg writing here conceived as being 'about the power to survive, not on the basis of original innocence, but on the basis of seizing the tools to mark the world that marked them as other' (ibid.: 175). Observing that 'writing is pre-eminently the technology of cyborgs' (ibid.: 176), and given her earlier comment about coding as the logic of the informatics of domination, she is thus able to conjure an affinity between feminist sci-fi cyborgs, in all their complex heterogeneity, and 'real-life cyborgs', such as 'the Southeast Asian village women workers in Japanese and US electronics firms' who are 'actively rewriting the texts of their bodies and societies'.

And she rehearses the key issue about dualisms as a way of knowing. We have used them in the West to order things, in a simple binary logic. Everything is either this, or not-this, with no room for in-betweens: 'self / other, mind / body, culture / nature, male / female, civilized / primitive' and so on (ibid.: 177). Western modernity has been all about this ordering and tidying up, and science has had a lead role to play in helping us collect, name and classify anything and everything (Latour 1993). The trouble is, technoscience has also led to the blurring of these binaries; as we find out more about the world, or come up with new marvels, so we undermine the simplicity of the binary classes. 'High-tech culture', Haraway says, 'challenges these dualisms in intriguing ways' (ibid.: 177). Cyborgs epitomize that intriguing trouble; they are irreducible back to one thing or another; instead of either / or, they are neither / both.

After tracking cyborgs in a selection of feminist science fiction texts, showing how they 'make very problematic the statuses of man or woman, human, artefact, member of a race, individual entity, or body' (ibid.: 178), Haraway moves towards her finale, with its famous, often-quoted phrases and ideas (I for one know this bit almost off by heart). First comes this intense set of statements:

> There are several consequences to taking seriously the imagery of cyborgs as other than our enemies. Our bodies, ourselves; bodies are maps of power and identity. Cyborgs are no exception. A cyborg body is not innocent; it was not born in a garden; it does not seek unitary identity and so generate antagonistic dualisms without end (or until the world ends); it takes irony for granted. One is too few, and two is only one possibility. Intense pleasure in skill, machine skill, ceases to be a sin, but an aspect of embodiment. The machine is not an *it* to be animated, worshipped, and dominated. The machine is us, our processes, an aspect of our embodiment. We can be responsible for machines; *they* do not dominate or threaten us. We are responsible for boundaries; we are they.
>
> (Haraway 1991: 180, emphasis in original)

Here is cyborg myth, cyborg gender, the cyborg reimagined away from militarism and the informatics of domination. 'We' *are* 'they': the categories blur and meld, 'the machine is us'. Sofoulis (2002) comments that this last segment of the Manifesto has often been misunderstood and misquoted in a decontextualized fashion, shorn of its socialist-feminist fuzz and buffed up to a shiny technophilia; certainly, as we shall see, the afterlives of Haraway's cyborg have taken it every which way, though this is in some senses inevitable – as Haraway (1995: xix) herself comments, 'cyborgs do not stay still'.

Here she is trying to story the world otherwise, to say that the cyborg is here, is us, but that we can do more than accept this on the terms of technoscience and the military – industrial complex. And returning finally to the question of feminism, as theory and politics, she comes to her famous summation. First, totalizing theory 'misses most of reality, probably always, but certainly now'. Second, it is inadequate to take up an anti-science and anti-technology standpoint – it is vital to find ways to work *with and against* science and technology, and here is where the cyborg can help us:

> Cyborg imagery can suggest a way out of the maze of dualisms in which we have explained our bodies and our tools to ourselves. This is a dream not of a common language, but of a powerful infidel heteroglossia. It is an imagination of a feminist speaking in tongues to strike fear into the circuits of the super-savers of the new right. It means both building and destroying machines, identities, categories, relationships, space stories. Though both are bound in the spiral dance, I would rather be a cyborg than a goddess.
>
> (Haraway 1991: 181)

Cyborg feminism – for some an uncomfortable, even oxymoronic term – is thus conjured here as a powerful force; powerful in its denial of dualisms, in its deployment rather than rejection of cyborg imagery, such as pleasure in machine skill, but still powerfully feminist. While this means rejecting the totalizing ideas of 'goddess feminism', it summons a resonant political alternative to challenge the informatics of domination. The rejection of previous articulations of feminism, goddess or radical or difference based, should not be misread as a rejection of feminism; far from it. This is not – or rather *not only* – the male cyborg of militarism or Hollywood. Indeed, in an interview Haraway insists that her cyborg is female:

> [The cyborg] is a polychromatic girl ... the cyborg is a bad girl, she is really not a boy. Maybe she is not so much bad as she is a shape-changer, whose dislocations are never free. She is a girl who's trying not to become Woman, but remain responsible to women of many colors and positions, and who hasn't really figured out a politics that makes the necessary articulations with the boys who are your allies. It's undone work.
>
> (Penley and Ross 1991: 20)

So the irony is in taking the cyborg, whether a vivisected lab rat fitted for space flight, or the *tech-noir* fantasies of hypermasculine Terminators and Blade Runners, and turning them into something politically potent, feminist and progressive: 'cyborgs for earthly survival!' (Haraway 1995) As Schneider (2005: 66) sums up, 'Multiplicities. Heterodoxies. Monstrosities. Improbable but promising couplings made by choice and based on assumed short-term common ends as well as means. These are the marks of Haraway's cyborg as a figure to think and live with'.

GODDESS FEMINISM

Also known as thealogy, contemporary goddess feminism emerged alongside so-called 'second wave' feminism, in the 1970s, and it remains a thriving global movement with a number of variants. Often connected to **ecofeminism**, a branch of feminism stressing women's connection to the natural environment, and to the idea of the Earth goddess, it combines spiritualism, ecologism and feminism centred on the goddess as a symbol of life, natural energy and female essence. The goddess is seen as a healer of the broken bonds between human and nature, body, Earth and cosmos, and as a symbol of fecundity.

SUMMARY

The Cyborg Manifesto was written 'as a somewhat desperate effort in the early Reagan years to hold together impossible things that all seemed true and necessary simultaneously' (Haraway 2004a: 3), a response to a request to account for the fate and future of socialist feminism in this 'new world order'. Haraway summoned the cyborg as a boundary blurring trickster figure, working to undermine the dualisms which have hitherto structured how we think and live. Aware of the cyborg's implication in what she calls the informatics of domination, and equally mindful of the trap of totalization which had arguably dead-ended feminist theory and politics at the time, she draws on an unlikely grab-bag of resources in an attempt to think the cyborg otherwise, as a figure of irony but also of hope.

2 CYBORG INVOCATIONS

Exuberant, expansive, perhaps over-responsible, and certainly ambitiously syn-
thetic, with its own suggestive flaws and fissures, the chimerical assemblage of
elements that is Haraway's Manifesto was capable of bearing many readings by
highly divergent audiences.

(Sofoulis 2002: 91)

Resisting the idea that she has somehow spawned a monster with a life of
its own, even though saying at one point that 'as an oppositional figure the
cyborg has a rather short half-life' (Markussen, Olesen and Lykke 2003:
52), Haraway remains doggedly committed to her cyborg, now enfolded
into a menagerie, or bestiary, or litter of figurations along with, among
others, OncoMouse™, FemaleMan©, *Mixotricha paradoxa*, vampire, gene,
chip, database, dog. In this section I want to track some of these subsequent manifestations, in her own and others' work – for this is not just
about diverse readings, but also diverse cyborg rewritings, diverse invoca-
tions of the cyborg. As Clough and Schnieder (2001: 345) say, 'Haraway's
figure of the cyborg ... has spawned countless clones and there is yet no
end to its productivity'; it has 'managed to insinuate itself into diverse
discursive spaces' (Sofoulis 2002: 91), and we now have around us a
'gallery of cyborg incarnation' (Christie 1992: 195).

CYBORGOLOGY

Perhaps inevitably, this morphing and cloning of the cyborg has put the
figure to all kinds of work, a lot of it beyond what Haraway has imagined,
though she is generously supportive of much of the reworking of her
ideas, not wanting to stake a claim in 'ownership' of the cyborg as a tool
for thinking: 'These young feminists', she comments in one interview,
'have truly rewritten the manifesto in ways that were not part of my
intention, but I can see what they are doing'. She adds, 'I think it is a
legitimate reading, and I like it, but it really wasn't what I wrote'
(Markussen, Olesen and Lykke 2003: 51). She does, however, confess to
finding some of the readings and rewritings 'distressing', and to wanting
to refuse the idea of the cyborg as a 'meta-category'; but I guess that is
also an inevitable part of the cyborg's unfaithfulness, to slip and slide into

new contexts, new places and times. Here she is in another interview, *locating* the cyborg:

> I am very concerned that the term 'cyborg' be used specifically to refer to those kinds of entities that became historically possible around World War II and just after. The cyborg is intimately involved in specific histories of militarization, of specific research projects with ties to psychiatry and communications theory, behavioral research and psychopharmacological research, theories of information and information processing. It is essential that the cyborg is seen to emerge out of such a specific matrix.
>
> (Haraway with Goodeve 2000: 129)

So, while Schneider (2005: 21) writes that she has been 'trying to avoid being misread while knowing that is, finally, impossible', Haraway has found herself, her cyborg and her Manifesto stitched into a range of debates about science, culture and society, some 'faithful' to these specificities, others not. And Haraway also confesses an unease at the 'celebrity' of her cyborg, but says that there is still worthwhile work to be done with this particular figuration: 'instead of giving up because it has become too famous, let's keep pushing and filling it' (Haraway with Goodeve 2000: 136).

Other writers have arguably done more that Haraway herself to police the cyborg's many new lives, to contain its celebrity. The Manifesto has catalysed a 'cyborg industry' in academia – birthing the field of 'cyborgology', as Gray, Figueroa-Sarriera and Mentor (1995) term it, itself part of the bigger explosion of interest in all things cyber. Cyborgology has indeed pushed and filled the cyborg, but not in ways that suit everyone's tastes. Bartsch, DiPalma and Sells (2001: 140), for example, argue that the cyborg has become overly 'literalized' in other theorists' hands, shedding its irony, its work as metaphor. They add that it now serves as 'the icon for a loose confederacy of cyborg scholars' who endlessly 'jockey the cyborg's currency' in academia. There is discomfort in some of the uses to which cyborg figuration is put, and a kind of squabbling over interpretations, over the 'faithfulness' of readings and rewritings which is understandable but also kind of ironic. Reviewing a number of these readings and rewritings, Sofoulis (2002) finds both consonant and dissonant texts, and a loose confederacy of divergent interpretations and critiques. She finds, for example, Judith Halberstam

(1991) connecting the cyborg to ideas about gender *as* technology; Sadie
Plant (1995) articulating a 'celebratory' woman-centred cyberfeminism;
Stacey Alaimo (1994) unable to reconcile the cyborg with ecofeminism,
and therefore jettisoning the former. Kathleen Woodward (1994) is seen
by Sofoulis as awkwardly oversimplifying the Manifesto's handling of
technology, while Nina Lykke (1996) rightly applauds its effects on feminist science studies, and Carol Stabile (1994) is found looking for the
wrong answers from the cyborg and as wrongly seeing the Manifesto as
political, unproductive and avant gardist. Anne Balsamo (1996) and Rosi
Braidotti (1994) receive more sympathetic treatment ... and so I could
go on.

This is part of the game that academics play, of course; interpreting
other people's ideas, critiquing other people's interpretations of other
people's ideas, working things over, so it's only to be expected. Cyborgs
don't stand still, remember. Part of this comes back to the issue of
timing: the Manifesto coincided with the turbulent period of postmodern
high theory and the necessary fragmenting of feminism, and it often thus
stands accused of becoming 'a widely accepted and largely unquestioned
orthodoxy of postmodern feminist thinking' (Currier 2003: 321) and as
opening up an unbridgeable rift between ecofeminism and cyborg or
postmodern feminism – though Haraway's later book *Modest_Witness* is
regarded as healing that rift (Scott 2001).

CYBORG KINSHIP

My world is sustained by queer confederacies.

(Haraway 2004b: 128)

Different parts of the Manifesto, different ways of thinking about the cyborg,
have been sampled and remixed, expanded or critiqued, by subsequent
writers from myriad different disciplines and orientations. The bloom in
cyborg publishing, cashing in on the cyborg's currency (in good and bad
ways), has brought us big compendiums like *The Cyborg Handbook* (Gray,
Figueroa-Sarriera and Mentor 1995) and *The Gendered Cyborg* (Kirkup, Janes,
Woodward and Hovenden 2000), the latter a graduate course reader evi-
dencing the spread of the cyborg into the classroom. We also have, among

countless others, books about *The Cyborg Experiments* in the art of Stelarc and Orlan (Zylinska 2002) and about the *Cyborg Citizen* in its myriad manifestations (Gray 2001), discussions of *Cyborg Babies* (Davis-Floyd and Dumit 1998), a title riffing on the closing phrase of the Manifesto, *Between Monsters, Goddesses and Cyborgs* (Lykke and Braidotti 1996), and so on. That last book invokes its three 'dubious creatures', all 'signifiers of chaos, heterogeneity and unstable identities' (Lykke 1996: 5), not to fold them together as doppelgangers, but to read them 'as a network of differing but unstably circulating meanings which inform current feminist dialogues and confrontations with science and technology' (ibid.). Others have similarly tried to keep cyborg and goddess in productive tension, refusing the choice that Haraway (with irony) makes, seeing goddesses *as* cyborgs (see Graham 1999, 2002). And, in one of my favourite asides, that also riffs on that closing phrase, Haraway responds to an interview question with 'I would rather go to bed with a cyborg than a sensitive man' (Penley and Ross 1991: 18).

Monsters, goddesses and cyborgs do have some kind of connection, some kind of kinship, of course. And Haraway has long been interested in the ideas of kinship, relationality, affinity; she has wanted to find different ways of thinking about connections and relations that aren't based on bloodline and family, in part to sidestep the pitfalls of psychoanalysis invoked to think the family in theory and in therapy, as well as to avoid the reductions of biologism – and also to arrive at a more open and productive set of encounters and coalitions which aren't about surrender, mastery or ownership, nor about totalizing identities, about two becoming one. Hence the cyborg mantra, *neither / both*, in place of either / or. This is an easy point to miss, however; some critics have written that the boundary transgressing of the cyborg depends on installing binaries to be transgressed (Kirby 1997), that Haraway can't help reifying the categories she uses her cyborg to smash. But I think this misses the bigger point and is little more than language games.

As already noted, one aspect of cyborg kinship that can be seen as troubling is the kinship of other types of cyborg, those that don't 'fit' with the Manifesto's dreamwork. As Elaine Graham (2002: 210) says, 'Haraway cannot claim a monopoly on cyborgs' – not that she'd want to – 'or assume that they are innocent of contrary readings'. She adds that Haraway's invocation of the cyborg 'cannot remain uncontaminated by other representations circulating in popular culture' (ibid.: 208), including many that work against the spirit of the Manifesto. Anne Balsamo (2000 [1988]), Mark Oehlert (1995) and Jennifer Gonzalez (2000 [1995]) all track popular culture's cyborgs, finding in some an echo of the promises of Haraway, but in others 'limiting, not liberating, gender sterotypes', especially when it comes to tracking 'cyborg women' (Balsamo 2000 [1988]: 155). But, remember how Haraway stresses the non-innocence of the cyborg, its blasphemy and unfaithfulness. So I think that unruly kin have to be seen as part of the cyborg's network: cyborgs don't stand still, and they don't always do what you want them to do. They are, as she would say later, 'bumptious'.

Haraway herself soon became mindful of this issue, arguing that cyborgs will always be changing, be changelings: 'already in the few decades that they have existed, they have mutated, in fact and fiction, into second-order enti-ties like genomic and electronic databases and other denizens of the zone called cyberspace' (Haraway 1995: xix). But she is also aware of the sen-sible limits of cyborg figuration, preferring to see the cyborg as one of the litter, along with 'many sorts of entities that are neither nature nor culture' (Markussen, Olesen and Lykke 2003: 57). Hence she arrives at the term 'a kinship of feminist figurations' (Haraway 2004a), made up of, as she puts it, 'florid, machinic, organic, and textual entities with which we share the earth and our flesh. These figures are full of bumptious life' (ibid.: 1). By now echoing Lykke and Braidotti as well as reworking her own earlier formulations, in this kin group she sees 'cyborgs and goddesses working for earthly survival' (ibid.: 3), and not just them, too: primates, coyotes, *Mixotricha paradoxa*, vampires, OncoMouse™ and FemaleMan©, dogs and dog people, and the famous list of figurations she gives in *Modest_Witness* (though she was then still calling them 'cyborg figures'): 'seed, chip, gene, database, bomb, fetus, race, brain, and ecosystem', products of global technoscience 'shocked into being from the force of the implosion of the natural and the artificial, nature and culture, subject and object, machine and organic body, money and lives, narrative and reality' (Haraway 1997: 12, 14). Developing her kinship thesis later in *Modest_Witness*, she writes:

I am sick to death of bonding through kinship and 'the family,' and I long for
models of solidarity and human unity and difference rooted in friendship, work,

partially shared purposes, intractable collective pain, inescapable mortality, and persistent hope.

(Haraway 1997: 265)

Let's take a couple of examples from her kin list, by way of illustration. First up, *Mixotricha paradoxa* (Haraway 1995, 2004b), which she discusses twice, as part of a confessional meditation on her own 'desire' for nature and her love of biology, and also as a kind-of cyborg, not least because knowledge of its existence and form is only enabled (for humans, at least) by the infrastructure of technoscience. *M. paradoxa* is a parasite that lives in the 'dark passages of a termite's gut' (Haraway 1995: xvi), from where its 'genre defying talents' have been observed thanks to 'all the material-izing instruments, discourses, and political economies of transnational technoscience – from scanning electron microscopes, to molecular genetic analysis, to theories of evolution, to circulations of money and people' (ibid.).

M. paradoxa is an extraordinary thing, a tiny 'hair' made up of assorted specialized micro-organisms living symbiotically or confederately. Here is Haraway's discussion of the significance of this parasite:

> *M. paradoxa* is a nucleated microbe with five distinct kinds of internal and external prokaryotic symbionts, including two species of motile spirochetes, which live in various degrees of structural and functional integration with the host. About one million 'individuals' of the five kinds of prokaryotes live with, on, and in the nucleated being that gets the generic name *Mixotricha*. ... When the congeries reach a couple of million, the host divides; and then there are two – or some power of ten to two. All the associated creatures live a kind of obligate confederacy. Opportunists all, they are nested in each other's tissues in a myriad of ways that make words like competition and cooperation, or individual and collective, fall into the trash heap of pallid metaphors and bad ontology.
>
> (Haraway 1995: xviii)

This tiny hair-like thing in the termite's hindgut, then, unsettles our 'normal' way of thinking about individuals and groups, and about rela-tionships; it 'interrogates individuality and collectivity at the same time' (Haraway with Goodeve 2000: 83). Even Haraway struggles with the words to describe what's going on here, with the relationship between

part and whole – is it 'it' or 'they'? I guess it's the cyborg answer: it's neither / both. And there are many other examples of such 'heterogeneous
associations', obligatory symbioses and loose-or-tight confederacies of
co-evolution and co-constitution. We are all of us bound in these kinds of
connections. Hence 'the relationship is the smallest possible unit of analysis' (Haraway 2003b: 77). And, in her most recent work, Haraway has
turned to a particular figuration of that unit of analysis.

COMPANION SPECIES

> I consider dog writing to be a branch of feminist theory, or the other way
> around.
>
> (Haraway 2003a: 3)

Over the last couple of years, Haraway has turned her attention towards
dogs and people, as a way 'to explore the layered meanings of historically
cohabiting companion species of many ontological kinds, organic and not'
(2004a: 5) – hence an explicit kin connection, right back to cyborgs. Yet
it would be a mistake to see the dog-person as a cyborg hybrid (though
see Michael 2000 for a suggestive similar reading of the 'hudogledog' –
the human + dog lead + dog). Or, as she puts it, 'the differences between
even the most politically correct cyborg and an ordinary dog matter',
adding that 'by the end of the millennium ... cyborgs could no longer do
the work of a proper herding dog to gather up the threads needed for
serious critical inquiry' (Haraway 2003b: 60). So, by her own omission,
she has 'gone to the dogs'. Importantly, dogs are material-semiotic entities; they are not metaphors, they are *dogs*, and 'they are not here just to
think with. They are here to live with. ... Dogs and people figure a universe' (Haraway 2003a: 5, 21). That universe, of course, is all about
naturecultures; the story of co-evolution and cohabitation, of dogs and
people, of relational domesticating, is all about 'otherness-in-connection'
(ibid.: 44). Dogs are not us, she insists, no matter how we anthropomor-
phize them. Using tales of her own life with dogs, as well as diverse
sources on dog–human relationships ranging from archaeozoology to
training manuals, Haraway explores the many ways that 'dogs are neither
nature nor culture, not both / and, not neither / nor, but something

else. … Dogs are very many kinds of entities' (Markussen, Olesen and Lykke 2003: 56, 55).

And, of course, companion species is a category much, much broader than dog worlds. Haraway is attuned to the specificities of dogs, to be sure, but also to understanding the broader implications of 'significant otherness', of how forms of relating between different material-semiotic entities get done. And she is aware that 'species' is a far-from-innocent concept, implicated in practices designed to ensure 'purity' – though she wants to keep the idea of species open to all kinds of entities (hence her choice of the term companion species over the more common but limiting 'companion animal'). Her 'Cyborgs to Companion Species' essay ends with a 'cat's cradle' listing twenty-one things Haraway likes about companion species, ending beautifully with 'A key question is: who cleans up the shit in a companion species relationship?' (Haraway 2003b: 79).

As part of this work she gives a reading of domestication and co-evolution of dogs and humans that stresses the relationality at work: people didn't simply decide to tame wolves to make them into dogs. What she calls 'dogs-to-be' worked at a way of relating with people that benefited both parties, as did the people: 'agency here is distributed, mobile, and complex', summarizes Schneider (2005: 85). And so it is today, in the many ways of relating between people and dogs: 'dogs are about the inescapable, contradictory story of relationships – co-constitutive relationships in which none of the partners pre-exist the relating, and *the relating is never done once and for all* ' (Haraway 2003a: 12, my emphasis). Although we have in some senses strayed a long way beyond our comfort zone in terms of this little book's focus in cyberculture – we too have gone to the dogs – it is hopefully clear why we have ended up here: cyborgs, Haraway has come to see, are 'junior siblings in the much bigger, queer family of companion species' (ibid.: 11), are all part of the same stories of technoscience and naturecultures.

SUMMARY

The Cyborg Manifesto catalysed a new field of cultural inquiry, cyborgology. People found cyborgs everywhere, doing all kinds of things – often things at odds with those described in the Manifesto. The Manifesto itself generated a lot of heat, and was installed at the core of this cyborgology. Haraway, meanwhile, was taking her cyborg in new directions, and introducing it to its 'queer kin', most recently by tracing a line from the cyborg to the companion species, and specifically to dog – human relationships. While not addressing the famous cartoon about identity masquerade on the Internet, 'In cyberspace no-one knows you're a dog', Haraway's work relocated the cyborg as part of this bigger kin group, all of whom in their own ways raise the question of what counts as nature and culture in our technoscientific world, and in the possibilities of more livable worlds.

3 CYBORG METHODS

To round off my discussion, I want to briefly focus on some recurring ideas in Haraway's work; these are ideas about method, about the way she approaches her units of analysis, about 'how to write theory … in order to find an absent, but perhaps possible, other present' (Haraway 1992: 295). But this isn't a discussion of method such as we might expect in social science, it isn't about sampling and such like. As we should by now expect from someone who confesses that she 'cannot *not* think through metaphor' (Haraway with Goodeve 2000: 86), Haraway uses a number of powerful devices to discuss her working method, but these too are often metaphorical: cat's cradle, diffraction. These are, of course, the most apposite methods with which to approach cyborgs. So, while Haraway confesses to finding 'words like "methodology" … very scary', preferring to talk of her 'ways of working' (ibid.: 82), a sketch map of cyborg methods will, I hope, help us understand those ways of working.

FIGURATION

If you've been reading attentively, you will have noticed that Haraway talks often of figuration. This notion, Sofoulis (2002) notes, is central to her method, and is most fully explicated in *Modest_Witness*, where she describes it as a 'contaminated practice' (Haraway 1997: 8). Figuration connects to another key notion I will try to explain in a moment, her discussion of 'material-semiotic entities'. But first to figuration, a concept that, Haraway writes, has 'deep roots in the semiotics of Western Christian realism' (ibid.: 9), in which the Old Testament is seen by the Christian Church as a prefiguring of events in the New Testament, as though the events described in the Old Testament, although they really happened, are allegorical and can be understood only by reference to the New Testament. So, in the context of Christian figural realism, the Old Testament is, in short, a figuration of the New Testament; the latter 'fulfils' the former, and there is a connection made between temporal meaning (history) and eternal meaning (a kind of retrospectively-read prophecy). Haraway detects this figural realism, and the Christian discourse around it, infusing technoscience in what she calls a 'barely secularized' form: 'In the United States, at least, technoscience is a millenarian discourse about beginnings and ends, first and last things, suffering and progress, figures and fulfillment' (Haraway 1997: 10).

This idea, then, immediately reminds us of Haraway's Catholic roots which, though she now calls herself anti-Catholic, nevertheless have left an indelible mark on her thinking, and which she mixes in with her other eclectic sources of inspiration. As Schenider (2005: 5) summarizes:

> One could safely say that her 'theory' [and I would add her method, too] is found primarily in her highly imaginative use of a range of metaphors and figures drawn from biology, feminism, Christianity, and science fiction; and often from all of these at once. Her narratives and their agents, dramas, and passions – even when they are somewhat fantastic – are always grounded in details of lived reality or embodied material at the same time that they invite us to think, act, and relate in hopeful ways that point beyond but intersect with these current 'real' local arrangements and practices toward new but also always 'real' possibilities. She has described this quality of her work as insisting on both the literal and the figural at the same time – something like literal / figural.
>
> (Schneider 2005: 5)

Of course, figuration, the figural, means others things, too, and Haraway is fully mindful of this matrix of meaning: the use of the term in analyses of rhetoric; the French meaning, face; figuring things out; figure meaning

an illustration or drawing ... (It is also a branch of sociology associated
with Norbert Elias.) So, she concludes:

> Figurations are performative images that can be inhabited. Verbal or visual, fig-
> urations can be condensed maps of contestable worlds. All language ... is fig-
> urative, that is, made of tropes, constituted by bumps that make us swerve
> from literal-mindedness. I emphasize figuration to make explicit and inescap-
> able the tropic quality of all material-semiotic processes, especially in techno-
> science.
>
> (Haraway 1997: 11)

This quote contains another of Haraway's favourite terms, trope. This also
has a number of meanings that nest together in her work: a trope is a
familiar or repeated term, symbol or character in a type or genre of literature (such as mad scientists in horror); it is also a figure of speech which
involves a play on words, such as metaphor or irony; and it is used in the
theory of history to account for the ways that different historians write
history – a use associated with the American academic Hayden White,
who hired Haraway at UCSC. So, lots of playful relationalities are at work
even in the words she chooses.

In conversation with Thyrza Nichols Goodeve, Haraway returns
repeatedly to her use of figuration, and to the tropic – to the folding of
the figural and the literal, 'the join between materiality and semiosis' or
the ways in which 'the literal and the figurative, the factual and the narrative, the scientific and religious and the literary, are all imploded'
(Haraway with Goodeve 2000: 86, 141). This implosion, so aptly tagged

SEMIOTICS

The so-called theory or science of signs, of how things mean. Described as 'the
single most important set of theoretical tools that is available to cultural studies'
(Edgar and Sedgwick 1999: 351), it has its origin in linguistics, and concerns the
links between things and words (signifiers) and meanings (signified). Signifier plus
signified equals sign, the thing and its meaning. To quote a suitably *canid* example
from a sociology dictionary: 'a photograph of a Rottweiler = dog = power, a fight-
ing dog = threat to children' (Jary and Jary 2000: 349).

by the many-meaning terms figuration and figure, is evident in her insistent conjoining of paired terms, most notably material-semiotic.

MATERIAL-SEMIOTIC

When Haraway says, as noted earlier, that dogs aren't metaphors, they are dogs, she is reminding us that they are, in fact, material-semiotic entities. To say that they are dogs doesn't mean to take the category 'dog' as self-evident and literal; it means to see dogs as concrete, or material, or fleshy things, but also as entities that mean things. Hence the material – the thingness of things – is welded to the semiotic (i.e. meaning).

But things aren't just what they mean, they are concrete, real things, too: a dog is a dog; although, as she says, 'dogs are many different kinds of entities' and 'the ontology of dogs turns out to be quite big' (Markussen, Olesen and Lykke 2003: 55). Hence, *material-semiotic* or, in Haraway's words, 'There's no place to be in the world outside of stories. ... Objects are frozen stories' (Haraway with Goodeve 2000: 107). She uses the term to discuss particular objects of knowledge, such as the gene, tracking at once 'how it is made to mean, and what is materially done to it or with it' (Sofoulis 2002: 88) – so there are material-semiotic actors, fields, practices, bodies, objects, worlds. Hence 'a gene is not a thing ... Instead, the term *gene* signifies a node of durable action where many actors, human and nonhuman, meet' (Haraway 1997: 142) – like the cyborg lab rat made by Clynes and Kline, or the tale of *Mixotricha paradoxa* told through technoscience, the gene is a recurrent figuration in Haraway's work. In fact, it is highlighted as one of two key figurations of the technoscientific present, along with the computer. As a central concept in Haraway's work, then, material-semiotic has echoes of naturecultures, not least in its insistence on conjoining or rejoining terms cleaved apart by a Western mindset stuck on binaries.

SITUATED KNOWLEDGES AND DIFFRACTION

Diffraction patterns record the history of interaction, interference, reinforcement, difference. Diffraction is about heterogeneous history ... Diffraction is a narrative, graphic, psychological, spiritual, and political technology for making consequential meanings.

(Haraway 1997: 273)

Over a number of years, Haraway has developed a perspective on the theories and methods of science studies. This is another vital strand to her work, but I cannot give it full treatment here, because it takes us too far from the cyborg – though, as I hope to suggest, there's something 'cyborgian' imprinted in her thinking here, too. The first key concept in this aspect of Haraway's work is 'situated knowledges', which she has worked through in relation to feminist science studies and in relation to teaching women's studies (Haraway 1992, 1997). It represents her attempt to bridge an impasse in feminist thought between so-called standpoint theory and postmodern or difference feminism, and it centres on the problematic notion of 'women's experience' as an analytical location.

In her essay 'Reading Buchi Emecheta: contests for "women's experience in women's studies"' (Haraway 1992/1988a), Haraway discusses feminist reading practices in relation to a Nigerian-born writer who emigrated to London in the 1960s. Using readings of Emecheta's work as a focus, her aim in this essay is to rethink the idea of 'women's experience' in the context of difference. Wanting to refuse the collapse into 'endless difference' (ibid.: 109) that she sees in postmodernism, Haraway wants to

FEMINIST STANDPOINT THEORY

Branch of feminist theory developed in the 1980s that argues that all knowledge is situated and produced from different standpoints or locations. Some knowledge is privileged, especially knowledge from oppressed or subjugated positions, because those in positions of power or authority cannot see the real conditions of domination and subordination. It draws on historical materialism within Marxism, that attempted to 'reveal' real class relations – the reality beneath appearances. So feminism can help women see the material conditions of gender oppression under which they live, and can thus activate change. Like much second-wave feminism, standpoint theory became fractured by vectors of difference that undermined any claim on a universal 'woman' or 'women's experience'.

articulate difference to politics and to the idea of accountability. So she begins to talk about 'situated knowledges' as a way of saying that knowledge is socially produced and so is related to experience and location, but not to say this means the 'anything goes' relativism that postmodern thinking gets tarred with. Crucially, and for some problematically, she highlights the situated knowledges of the oppressed or subjugated as particularly important:

> Situated knowledges are particularly powerful tools to produce maps of consciousness for people who have been inscribed within the marked categories of race and sex that have been so exuberantly produced in the histories of masculinist, racist, and colonialist dominations. Situated knowledges are always *marked* knowledges; they are re-markings, reorientations, of the great maps that globalized the heterogeneous body of the world in the history of masculinist capitalism and colonialism.
>
> (Haraway 1992/1988b: 111, emphasis in original)

In this formulation she is trying also to bridge feminist theory and 'the critical study of colonialist discourse', or what we might name postcolonial theory, by mapping how both 'intersect with each other in terms of two crucial binary pairs – that is, *local / global* and *personal / political*' (ibid.). And, through this, Haraway hopes to rethink the notion of 'women's experience' away from totalizing or universalizing, indeed away from identity and identity politics, and instead towards a politics built on affinity: local *and* global *and* personal *and* political. Her hope in this essay

SOCIAL CONSTRUCTIONISM

The idea that knowledge, facts, truth, even reality, are all constructed in a particular culture or society, rather than being pre-existing or natural. In science studies, social constructionism (sometimes called constructivism) argues that scientists are social actors, and that science is a social practice: rather than uncovering the truth, scientists construct it through the ways they think and work. The term is also more broadly applied in cultural studies and sociology, as the opposite of essentialism in work on identity for example – so the identity category 'woman' is a product of society, not pre-given or natural.

REFLEXIVITY

In social science studies, reflexivity was developed as a strategy to reveal the social construction of scientific knowledge and practice. It means interrogating the practices of science that give us certain ways of understanding the world (this is constitutive reflexivity as opposed to self-reflexivity). It also means interrogating the practices of science studies that give us a particular understanding of science. In particular, attention turns to the 'texts' that science produces – whether a paper or a chip or a gene – to understand how these in turn produce scientific knowledge (e.g. the structure of scientific articles delineates what counts and doesn't count as 'proper science').

is to find 'a space for political accountability and for cherishing ambiguities, multiplicities, and affinities without freezing identities' (ibid.: 121). So there is a clear connection here across to her work on cyborgs and companion species in this grappling with difference and affinity, as well as to Chela Sandoval's (1995) 'methodology of the oppressed' which influenced the Cyborg Manifesto.

These ideas she further elaborated in a parallel essay, 'Situated Knowledges: The Science Question in Feminism and the Privilege of Partial Perspective' (Haraway 1992/1988b). This piece resonated through a whole other series of debates, too, in terms of feminist science studies; it has been as impactful as the Cyborg Manifesto, in fact, across a range of disciplines trying to find ways to think about the researching, writing and reading practices generally framed by the notion of the social construction of knowledge.

In this engagement with science studies and especially feminist science studies, Haraway also critiqued the dominant methodological approach, reflexivity (see also Haraway 1997). Reflexivity here means 'an interrogation of the practices that frame our accounts of the world', including accounts called science and accounts *about* science (Campbell 2004: 163). Reflexivity is a way of getting at the idea that what counts as truth is socially constructed, and involves ways of reading and of writing that seek to reveal how knowledge is constructed. It has come to be an almost standard element of social studies of science, though still a hotly contested one. The problem with this approach for Haraway, according to Schneider (2005) is that it places too much emphasis on the semiotic, not enough on the material; given what we now know about her insistence on conjoining these two terms, I think Schneider is right.

The development of this kind of thinking in feminist science studies has a slightly different trajectory, but arguably retains a greater sense of the politics at work here, connecting science studies back out from the laboratory to the world, to gender issues: '[feminist science studies] often has strong reasons to argue that the fiction of gender that science presents is not merely less persuasive but less accurate' (Campbell 2004: 167) – hence Haraway's insistence on objectivity.

As with 'Reading Buchi Emecheta', there is also here an engagement with postmodern thinking, an attempt not to succumb to the 'play of signifiers' and language games. And this engagement is about politics: 'the further I get with the description of the radical social constructionist programme and a particular version of postmodernism, the more nervous I get' (Haraway 1992/1988b: 185). She particularly wants to hold onto something that had become a dirty word in constructionist thinking: the notion of objectivity, derived from Marxist feminism and central to standpoint theory. But she finds both postmodern constructionism and standpoint theory limited and limiting, and strives to think situated knowledges as a way of moving beyond this impasse too:

> So, I think my problem and 'our' problem is how to have simultaneously an account of radical historical contingency for all knowledge claims and knowing subjects, a critical practice for recognizing our own 'semiotic technologies' for making meanings, and a no-nonsense commitment to faithful accounts of a 'real' world, one that can be partially shared and friendly to earth-wide projects of finite freedom, adequate material abundance, modest meaning in suffering, and limited happiness.
>
> (Haraway 1992/1988b: 187)

A notion of feminist objectivity emerges here as situated knowledge, embodied and located. Knowledge is produced in networks of 'actants', human and nonhuman, in particular circumstances and particular configurations or relationalities: 'in a differentiated social space, different social positions will produce different knowledges' (Campbell 2004:

171) – but not just flatly different: some are better, more accurate, than others: 'a knower occupying a social position of subjugation will provide a more accurate knowledge of oppressive social relations' (ibid.). So a situated reflexivity here aims to hold onto the promises of reflexivity but to reinforce the location from which that reflexivity comes, always with a political imperative.

Now, to find a way to think this through, Haraway offers the idea of diffraction to replace the reflection audible in reflexivity:

> Reflexivity has been much recommended as a critical practice, but my suspicion is that reflexivity, like reflection, only displaces the same elsewhere … Reflexivity is a bad trope for escaping the false choice between realism and relativism in thinking about strong objectivity and situated knowledges in technoscientific knowledge. What we need is to make a difference in material-semiotic apparatuses, to diffract the rays of technoscience so that we get more promising interference patterns on the recording films of our lives and bodies.
>
> (Haraway 1997: 16)

Stressing that diffraction is for her 'a metaphor for the effort to make a difference in the world' (ibid.), Haraway sees it as a way to intervene in the networks of actants to produce both new actants (which she also refers to as 'inappropriate/d others') and new networks. Diffraction is an oppositional practice 'in which we learn to think our political aims from the *analytic and imaginative standpoint* of those existing in different networks to those of domination' (Campbell 2004: 175).

Diffraction for Haraway is also about different reading practices interacting – reading a scientific paper or reading a poem, for example – connecting us back to her work on Buchi Emecheta and, indeed, her work on primatology. As she elaborates in an interview with Joseph Schneider, 'Different reading skills interact diffractively. I know the difference between one set of skills and another, but they constantly interrupt each other productively. They produce jokes, so that what appears to be straightforward gets bent in interesting ways' (Schneider 2005: 149). She exemplifies this through one of her favourite resources, science fiction, and a comment by writer Samuel Delaney that the phrase 'Her world exploded' means one thing in 'ordinary literature' – it suggests some kind of psychological breakdown or whatever – while in science fiction it might mean literally that the character's world, her home planet, blew up. The juxtaposition between those two readings is diffraction. So diffraction patterns register interference, how things are changed in interaction, thus figuring for Haraway the strong objectivity of situated knowledges and ways of relating and interacting that produce patterns of difference. Such ways of relating and patterns are also conjured in the last 'cyborg method' I want to talk about here, cat's cradle.

CAT'S CRADLE

The 'string-on-fingers' game of cat's cradle is offered by Haraway as a better way to understand the practices of science, and thus as a 'method' for science studies, in place of more adversarial metaphors of struggle and battle (Haraway 1994, 1997; see also Schneider 2005). Cat's cradle is relational, attentive and embodied; it is about knots and patterns, and the game is best played collectively, passing the cradle from one person's hands to another, making more and more patterns, complex and changing: 'one person can build up a large repertoire of string figures on a single pair of hands, but the cat's cradle figures can be passed back and forth on the hands of several players, who add new moves in the building of complex patterns' (Haraway 1997: 268). Moreover, there is no 'winner' in this game, no final score: 'the goal is more interesting and open-ended than that' (ibid.). The fun of producing knots and patterns, of figuring out how certain moves made certain knots (though not always possible), represents an 'embodied analytical skill' (ibid.), echoing her discussion of pleasure in machine skill for cyborgs. It is, Haraway says to Goodeve, 'methodology with a small "m". It's a way of working and a way of thinking about work', adding that it was addressed by her 'to science studies people to draw more thickly from feminist studies and cultural studies and vice versa', and that it's also how teaching should be (Haraway with Goodeve 2000: 156). Played all over the world, cat's cradle is 'both local and global, distributed and knotted together' (Haraway 1997: 268), hence figuring for Haraway a possible new way of knotting together 'the varying threads of science studies, antiracist feminist theory, and cultural studies' (ibid.). As an image and a practice to end on, nothing seems more appropriate than this passed-between-hands, strings-on-fingers game of patterns and knots.

SUMMARY

Throughout her work, Haraway attempts to find new ways of thinking and writing about the world as it is, and about possible, more 'livable' worlds. Her work is marked by a deep political commitment, borne out in her working methods. The key concepts discussed here – figuration, material-semiotic, situated knowledges, diffraction, cat's cradle – do not represent a 'cyborg toolkit' for how to 'do a Haraway'; rather they should be seen as parts of an ongoing working-through of how to talk about 'elsewhere'. The interference patterns that diffraction produces, the knotty webs of cat's cradle, the strong objectivity that situated knowledges promise, and the insistence on understanding figurations of material-semiotic entities as 'frozen stories', are themselves knotted threads, passed back and forth, still producing surprising patterns.

AFTER HARAWAY

Speaking as a multicellular, eukaryotic, bilaterally symmetrical confederacy, a fish, in short, I want to learn to strike up interesting intercourse with possible subjects about livable worlds.

(Haraway 2004b [1992])

Haraway's turn to dogs and dog people gives us a heads-up on what we can expect next. In recent interviews she sees 'dog studies' as a fruitful place to continue her work, satisfying her love of biology and her yearning for possible elsewheres. Of course, her 'celebrity' status means that 'dog studies' may soon feel the bright light of attention in the same way that 'cyborg studies' did in the cyberquake of the Cyborg Manifesto.

So dogs join the queer kin group that Haraway gathers around her. As well as the figurations of those kin, there are of course other kindred networks to think about, most notably perhaps the network of scholars who have worked with Haraway, especially the students whose work she always so generously refers to, and from whom she has so obviously learnt so much in the cat's cradle of teaching and learning. Among the many, Zoë Sofoulis, Chela Sandoval, Chris Gray, Katie King and Thyrza Goodeve have all produced work knotted with Haraway's, passed between hands. And of course, there are those countless others who have taken something from her work onto their own fingers, even if Haraway is sometimes surprised – and not always positively – by the patterns they produce.

The cyborg is perhaps most emblematic of this: a figuration born in a particular place and time, tasked to do particular work, that has lived on, morphed and mutated. There seemed to be a time when Haraway rued the day she had talked about the cyborg, and she was unhappy about its 'celebrity' status. Now she has found a home for it, and some littermates. The cyborg will live on, in her hands and in others, despite (ironically) requiring 'an awful lot of intervention in order to survive ... It has to be technically enhanced to survive in this world' (Markussen, Olesen and Lykke 2003: 57). What will also live on is Haraway's attempt to keep feminist and antiracist political commitment at the heart of what we might now call 'critical technoscience studies', and equally her commitment to technoscience as a site of possibilities. As Myerson writes, commenting on *Modest_Witness*, we do not get easy answers from Haraway; instead, 'We leave Haraway with a more focused sense of the real ambiguity of things, an ambiguity which will have to be part of any answers that we choose to give, any commitments we make' (Myerson 2000: 68).

AFTER CYBERCULTURE

If you cast your mind back to my discussion of Manuel Castells, you may remember his allergy to futurology. I share at least some of his symptoms, yet at the same time I must confess to finding something thrilling in speculations about the future, especially those concerning technology (on the troubled history and tricky business of futurology, see Margolis 2000). A few months ago, one of the UK's Sunday newspapers launched a new technology supplement, full of sumptuous photos of shiny new gadgets, and commenting on new trends in use (women as the new geeks, the rise of cameraphones making all of us potential paparazzi), including a feature on people employed to conjure the future, prophets who eye current trends and dream their extrapolation. I feel like I am being asked to join their ranks here – and I feel a mix of excitement and dread: writing a book about cyberculture means writing about a present that will already be the past by the time you're reading this, or writing a future that may not happen. Or, As William Gibson put it, in a quote from the Sunday supplement, 'The future has already happened, it just isn't very well distributed' (quoted in Anderson 2005: 49). The trickiness of prediction and the embarrassments of hindsight mean that this part of the book should be read as a time-capsule.

Looking backwards to look forwards is a way of handling the uncertainties of futurology; a process I have previously described as 'technostalgia', or the gap between the present as it was imagined in the past as the future, and the present as it is. Such an exercise was carried out by Leah Lievrouw (2004) on behalf of the journal *New Media & Society*, to mark the fifth anniversary of its founding. She commissioned a number of essays and commentaries on the past, present and future of new media and new media studies, starting with her own overview. When the journal was launched, she writes, the world wide web was still in its infancy, web browsers were only just beginning to change web use, the dot.com boom was booming and seemingly unstoppable, the digital divide was only emerging as a concern, overshadowed by fears of the Millennium bug. Her message is: things change, things stay the same. Unforeseen developments and unforeseen problems have materialized since 1999, predictions have both come true and been proven false. Dot.coms went bust, the bug wasn't the end of the world, the Internet has become part of our lives in ways both foreseen and unforeseen.

Indeed, one crucial change since the end of the twentieth century that Lievrouw and her contributors remark upon is the 'mainstreaming' of the Internet; its 'banalization'. Gibson's comment about the future not being very well distributed has been replaced with the ubiquity – for those on the right side of the digital divide – of cyberculture. Shopping, education, entertainment, socializing, politics, work are all 'networked' to varying degrees and in varying ways, and many people's experiences of those activities have been utterly transformed in the process.

At the start of this book I tried to capture the breadth and diversity of things that I collect under the banner cyberculture. I noted how other people choose to call this loose collective something else – Lievrouw prefers to talk of new media, others like digital culture, and so on. That breadth and diversity (including in its naming) is part of the thrill and part of the problem of prediction: the sheer variety (and unpredictability) of forms, content, platforms, devices, applications – and their manifold convergences – makes the landscape of cyberculture very complex. Content migrates between devices, devices change shape in our hands; yet some parts of that landscape have more-or-less stabilized: the personal computer is, for most of us, still a keyboard, mouse, monitor and 'tower'. But remember also that some seriously believed predictions, such as the 'death' of the city, simply haven't come true: there is stabilization in some things that were supposed to be utterly changed by cyberculture. So, when I said just a moment ago that work has been transformed by being networked, which I do believe to be true, I should add that it hasn't been transformed in the ways that were being predicted a decade or so ago. We don't all telework – though more of us do something like that, at least some of the time. But networked computers have become an everyday, banal part of many people's working lives, even those whose jobs are far, far away from computing.

The futurologists interviewed in my Sunday supplement noted that use is possibly the hardest thing to predict: how people will live with technologies, which applications they will take up, which they will adapt, which they will find useless or unnecessary. Cyberculture is intensely creative, putting devices and applications to new uses, selectively adopting and adapting the forms, content and uses provided. Last night, for example, I went to hear a talk about 'flashmobbing' – a kind of political art pranking using websites and mobile phones to coordinate a group of people to assemble at a particular place – often in commercial space, such as a shopping centre – to perform a seemingly pointless, surreal collective action. While the motives and meanings of flashmobbing seem wilfully uncertain, and while it has already begun to fade as an activity, such countercultural uses of new technologies will surely blossom in unpredictable ways in the future.

Countercultural uses of new technologies have, of course, long been a site of interest for cyberculture theorists. From Castells' work on grassrooting the space of flows to recent work on 'hacktivism', which 'draws on the creative use of computer technology for the purposes of facilitating online protests, performing civil disobedience in cyberspace and disrupting the flow of information by deliberately intervening in the networks of global capital' (Gunkel 2005: 595), such uses remind us of the creativity of users very vividly. Of course, non-countercultural uses also proliferate and diversify – text messaging is an obvious example, or listening to music stored as MP3 files on iPods. And, to go back to my work example, I see on a daily basis how the commuter train has become for many people a collective mobile office, as they carry out work activities on their laptops, mobiles, BlackBerrys, PDAs. The banalization of cyberculture is evident in these everyday, taken-for-granted uses (which are, of course, nonetheless truly remarkable). As Lievrouw (2004: 11) adds, this also means that 'users' expectations about [new media] have become at once more expansive and more routine'.

What does this all mean for the academic study of cyberculture? Well, aside from making it an anxious enterprise, given the intense time-sensitivity of the topic, it also makes it very exciting; there are always new things to think with, and new ways of thinking them with. Cyberculture theory is, in a way, also at once expansive and routine – expansive in its coverage and in the theories and methods it uses, routine in that it has become an established area of academic work in its own right, as evidenced by courses, jobs and research and publications, all of which still bloom. Despite such blooming and such branching, moreover, there have been broad discernible trends in the development of cyberculture studies, such as the three stages outlined by Silver (2000) and discussed in the introduction of this book. The stage we're at now, which Silver names 'critical cyberculture studies', is described by Lievrouw (2004: 12) as a turn to the 'interior', to the personal experience of cyberculture, 'dominated by micro-scale, social constructivist approaches, opposition to technological determinism, and ethnographic methodologies' – exactly the approach sketched here via Bakardjieva's work (and prefigured in Turkle's).

Now, while Lievrouw is supportive of this approach, she also notes that it has to some extent obscured 'large-scale social, political and economic developments, technological changes, and structures of power that do in fact constrain (if not determine) how ICTs are designed and used' (ibid.: 13). This, I think, is where the work of Castells and Haraway can be helpful, in using both macro and micro approaches, in always pointing up the bigger picture and the big issues.

So, finally, what are these big issues? One that both Haraway and Castells discuss is the commingling of cyberculture with biotechnologies, as in the mapping of the human genome, or the production of transgenic organisms, or work that fuzzes the boundaries between bio and tech, such as nanoscience. Then there's the big issue already noted: what we might call, using a seemingly old-fashioned term, the political economy of cyberculture – questions of power, ownership, inequality, domination. Sometimes we need to reuse old tools to think things anew with, while at other times we will need new approaches – approaches as yet unforeseen – to think with, as the landscape of cyberculture constantly shifts. My aim here has been modest, then: to provide some tools to think with, to aid in navigation. In the end, I want to echo Maria Bakardjieva's (2005: 198) closing words, in the hope of encouraging you to set off across that landscape, to find your own way: 'everything is still at stake'.

FURTHER READING

WORKS BY CASTELLS

This annotated list includes the main books written or co-written by Castells that are discussed here, plus some of the articles and chapters that elaborate the main themes of *The Information Age*, some published interviews, and a selection of critical appraisals. A more lengthy bibliography, with accompanying biography, can be found in Castells and Ince (2003).

Castells, M. (1972) *The Urban Question: A Marxist Approach*, London: Arnold.
Castells' first major work in urban sociology, showing his indebtedness to Marxist approaches to understanding the social and economic geography of cities.

Castells, M. (1983) *The City and the Grassroots: A Cross-cultural Theory of Urban Social Movements*, London: Arnold.
Definitive and highly influential study of social movement politics in San Francisco.

Castells, M. (1989) *The Informational City: Information Technology, Economic Restructuring and the Urban – regional Process*, Oxford: Blackwell.
Begins to develop ideas fleshed out in *The Information Age*, such as the space of flows, via an analysis of the changing regional industrial geography of the USA.

Castells, M. and Hall, P. (1994) *Technopoles of the World: The Making of 21st Century Industrial Complexes*, London: Routledge.
Co-written survey of new 'milieux of innovation' in major city-regions worldwide.

Castells, M. (1996a / 2000) *The Information Age: Economy, Society and Culture. Volume 1: The Rise of the Network Society*, Oxford: Blackwell.
The first volume of the trilogy, laying out key ideas such as the network society and the culture of real virtuality.

Castells, M. (1996b) 'The net and the self: working notes for a critical theory of the informational society', *Critique of Anthropology* 16(1): 9 – 37.
A run-through of the main ideas in *The Information Age*, focusing especially on issues of identity.

Castells, M. (1997/2004) *The Information Age: Economy, Society and Culture. Volume 2: The Power of Identity*, Oxford: Blackwell.
Second volume, focusing on cultural social movements, uses of identity to articulate resistance to the network society, and the changing role of nation-states and party politics.

Castells, M. (1998/2000) *The Information Age: Economy, Society and Culture. Volume 3: End of Millennium,* Oxford: Blackwell.
Covers the collapse of statism, the new Fourth World, the global criminal economy, and rounds off the trilogy with a conclusion and some (rare) futurology.

Castells, M. (1999) 'Grassrooting the space of flows', *Urban Geography* 20(4): 294 – 302 [published in a slightly different form in J. Wheeler, Y. Aoyama and B. Warf (eds) (2000) *Cities in the Telecommunications Age*, London: Routledge, pp. 18 – 27].
Offers a corrective to Castells' earlier view that withdrawing to 'cultural communes' was the only countercultural response to the network society; he shows here how social movements of various types make use of networks.

Castells, M. (2000a) 'Information technology and global capitalism', in W. Hutton and A. Giddens (eds) *On the Edge: Living with Global Capitalism*, London: Jonathan Cape, pp. 52 – 74.
Focuses on the economic geographies of the network society.

Castells, M. (2000b) 'Materials for an exploratory theory of the network society', *British Journal of Sociology* 51(1): 5 – 24.
Describes the 'social morphology' of the network society, rehearsing some of the main arguments of volumes 1 and 2 of the trilogy.

Castells, M. (2001a) 'Epilogue: informationalism and the network society', in P. Himanen, *The Hacker Ethic and the Spirit of the Information Age*, London: Secker & Warburg.
Uses the epilogue to Himanen's essay on hacking to show the special role of hackers in the formation and contestation of the network society.

Castells, M. (2001b) *The Internet Galaxy: Reflections on the Internet, Business, and Society*, Oxford: Oxford University Press.
Based on the 2000 Clarendon Lectures in Management at the University of Oxford, this gives accessible accounts of the role of the Internet in the network society.

Castells, M. and Catterall, B. (2001) *The Making of the Network Society*, London: ICA.
Transcript of an interview which crystallizes the main points of *The Information Age*.

Castells, M. (2002 [1996]) 'An introduction to the information age', in G. Bridge and S. Watson (eds) *The Blackwell City Reader*, Oxford: Blackwell, pp. 125 – 34 [originally published in *City* 7: 6 – 16].
An excellent summary of *The Information Age*, based on a lecture, and more polemical than some of his other writing.

Castells, M. and Ince. M. (2003) *Conversations with Manuel Castells*, Cambridge: Polity.
A series of interviews that give good insight into Castells' life and work.

Roberts, J. (2004 [1999]) 'Theory, technology and cultural power: an interview with Manuel Castells', in F. Webster and B. Dimitriou (eds) *Manuel Castells*, London: Sage, pp. 328 – 35 [originally published in *Angelaki* 4(2): 33 – 9].
A short interview discussing the main ideas of *The Information Age*.

Castells, M. (2005) 'Space of flows, space of places: materials for a theory of urbanism in the information age', in B. Sanyal (ed.) *Comparative Planning Cultures*, New York: Routledge, pp. 45 – 63.

Castells is also series editor for *The Information Age Series*, published by Blackwell, self-described as 'the Nasdaq of the social sciences', which publishes empirically informed analyses of dimensions of the network society, including volumes by former graduate students. They are thus important nodes in the 'Castells network'. The series has so far included the following:

Benner, C. (2002) *Work in the New Economy: Flexible Labor Markets in Silicon Valley*, Oxford: Blackwell.

Servon, L. (2002) *Bridging the Digital Divide: Technology, Community, and Public Policy*, Oxford: Blackwell.

Wellman, B. and Haythornwaite, C. (eds) (2002) *The Internet in Everyday Life*, Oxford: Blackwell.

Zoon, M. (2004) *The Geography of the Internet Industry*, Oxford: Blackwell.

WORKS ABOUT CASTELLS

Only those critical works referred to in the text are cited here. For an extensive collection of critiques, see Webster and Dimitriou (2004).

Ince, M. (2004 [2000]) 'Uneasy? He's here to help', in F. Webster and B. Dimitriou (eds) *Manuel Castells*, London: Sage, pp. 325 – 7 [originally published in *Times Higher Education Supplement*, 24 November: 11].
A short newspaper article introducing *The Information Age*.

McGuigan, J. (1999) *Modernity and Postmodern Culture*, Buckingham: Open University Press, ch. 5, 'The information age'.
A useful critical appreciation of the first two volumes of the trilogy.

Stalder, F. (1998) 'The network paradigm: social formations in the age of information', *The Information Society* 14: 301 – 8.
An incisive review essay of the trilogy that does a great job of condensing 1500 pages of Castells into just eight.

Van Dijk, J. (1999) 'The one-dimensional network society of Manuel Castells', *New Media & Society* 1(1): 127 – 38.
Good, critical review of *The Information Age*, highlighting what the reviewer sees as conceptual weaknesses, for example around causality and technological determinism.

Webster, F. (2002) *Theories of the Information Society*, 2nd edn, London: Routledge, ch. 5, 'Informational capitalism: Manuel Castells'.
Excellent overview and critical commentary, though less critical than some of Webster's other articles on Castells.

Webster, F. and Dimitriou, B. (eds) (2004) *Manuel Castells*, London: Sage (3 volumes).
A collection of critiques of Castells' main body of work; volumes 2 and 3 centre on *The Information Age* material, reprinting reviews and responses.

Webster, F. and Robins, K. (1998) 'The iron cage of the information society', *Information, Communication & Society* 1(1): 23 – 45.
Argues that there's more continuity than change in the information age, especially where capital and class are concerned.

WORKS BY HARAWAY

A full and up-to-date bibliography of Haraway's work can be found in Schneider (2005) – and there are also several on the web. Here I list the main publications discussed in this book, some of the published interviews (which offer an accessible insight into Haraway's work, life and sense of humour) and a selection of useful secondary works.

Haraway, D. (1976/2004) *Crystals, Fabrics, and Fields: Metaphors of Organicism in Twentieth-century Developmental Biology*, New Haven CT: Yale University Press [reprinted in 2004, with a new introduction, as *Crystals, Fabrics, and Fields: Metaphors that Shape Embryos*, Berkeley CA: North Atlantic Press].
Based on her PhD thesis, this book shows Haraway's ideas about science as culture taking shape; the new introduction situates it in the context of her later work.

Haraway, D. (1985) 'A manifesto for cyborgs: science, technology, and socialist feminism in the 1980s', *Socialist Review* 80: 65 – 108.

Her response to the question of the fate of socialist feminism under Reaganism – an ironic political myth. Also published, with revisions, in *Simians, Cyborgs, and Women* and *The Haraway Reader*.

Haraway, D. (1989) *Primate Visions: Gender, Race, and Nature in the World of Modern Science*, New York, Routledge.
A study of primatology's way of seeing apes, and humans, deepening Haraway's method of reading and writing science with a strong political edge.

Haraway, D. (1991) *Simians, Cyborgs, and Women: The Reinvention of Nature*, London: Free Association Books.
Collects many of the important articles written in the 1980s, with three sections: 'Natures as a system of production and reproduction', 'Contested readings: narrative natures' and 'Differential politics for inappropriate/d others'.

Haraway, D. (1991/1988a) 'Reading Buchi Emecheta: contests for "women's experience" in women's studies', in *Simians, Cyborgs, and Women: The Reinvention of Nature*, London: Free Association Books, pp. 109 – 24.

Haraway, D. (1992) 'The promises of monsters: a regenerative politics for inappropriate/d others', in L. Grossberg, C. Nelson and P. Treichler (eds) *Cultural Studies*, New York: Routledge, pp. 295 – 337 [also published in *The Haraway Reader*].

Haraway, D. (1991/1988b) 'Situated knowledges: the science question in feminism and the privilege of partial perspective', in *Simians, Cyborgs, and Women: the Reinvention of Nature*, London: Free Association Books, pp. 183 – 202.

Haraway, D. (1994) 'A game of cat's cradle: science studies, feminist theory, cultural studies', *Configurations* 2(1): 59 – 71.
Uses the metaphor of cat's cradle to suggest the unfinished, ever-changing intersections of these three ways of thinking about the world.

Haraway, D. (1995) 'Cyborgs and symbionts: living together in the new world order', in C. Gray (ed.) *The Cyborg Handbook*, London: Routledge.
Brilliant short discussion that moves between cyborg lab rats to the hind-gut of a termite, and many places in between.

Haraway, D. (1997) *Modest_Witness@Second_Millennium.Female Man©_ Meets_OncoMouse*™, New York: Routledge.

Haraway, D. (2003a) *The Companion Species Manifesto: Dogs, People, and Significant Otherness*, Chicago IL: Prickly Paradigm Press.
Haraway 'gone to the dogs', thinking the relationalities of dogs and their humans in all their complexity, as naturecultures.

Haraway, D. (2003b) 'Cyborgs to companion species: reconfiguring kinship in technoscience', in D. Idhe and E. Selinger (eds) *Chasing Technoscience: Matrix for Materiality*, Bloomington IN: Indiana University Press.
Charts her move towards the companion species manifesto, and from cyborgs to dogs and dog people. Also published in *The Haraway Reader*.

Haraway, D. (2004a)'Introduction: a kinship of feminist figurations', in D. Haraway (ed.) *The Haraway Reader*, New York: Routledge.
A great introduction to this collection of her 'greatest hits' – a great way into her work and her current preoccupations.

Haraway, D. (2004b [1992]) 'Otherworldly conversations; terran topics; local terms', in D. Haraway (ed.) *The Haraway Reader*, New York: Routledge [previously published in *Science as Culture* 3(1): 59 – 92].
She describes this as a 'confessional piece', taking back to her roots in biology, and to a parasite in a termite's hindgut.

Haraway, D. (ed.) (2004c) *The Haraway Reader*, New York: Routledge.
Nine key essays, a great interview, and a contextualizing introduction.

INTERVIEWS WITH HARAWAY

As I noted earlier, Donna Haraway 'gives good interview': these are excellent ways into her work, showing her humour, combining autobiography with theory, in an accessible, conversational style. All of these are highly recommended.

Gordon, A. (1994) 'Possible worlds: an interview with Donna Haraway', in M. Ryan and A. Gordon (eds) *Body Politics: Disease, Desire, and the Family*, Boulder CO: Westview.
Haraway, D. with Goodeve, T. (2000) *How Like a Leaf*, New York: Routledge.

Kunzru, H. (1998) 'You are cyborg', *Wired* 5(2): 1 – 8, available on-line at http://www.wired.com/archive//5.02/ffharaway.html (accessed 19 October 2005).

Markussen, R., Olesen, F. and Lykke, N. (2003) 'Interview with Donna Haraway', in D. Idhe and E. Selinger (eds) *Chasing Technoscience: Matrix for Materiality*, Bloomington IN: Indiana University Press. [Reprinted as the first part of Markussen, R., Olesen, F. and Lykke, N. (2004) 'Cyborgs, coyotes and dogs: a kinship of feminist figurations, and, There are always more things going on than you thought! Methodologies as thinking technologies', in D. Haraway (ed.) *The Haraway Reader*, New York: Routledge].

Penley, C. and Ross, A. (1991) 'Cyborgs at large: interview with Donna Haraway', in C. Penley and A. Ross (eds) *Technoculture*, Minneapolis MN: University of Minnesota Press.

Schneider, J. (2005) 'Conversations with Donna Haraway', in *Donna Haraway: Live Theory*, London: Continuum.

WORKS ABOUT HARAWAY

Balsamo, A. (2000 [1988]) 'Reading cyborgs writing feminism', in G. Kirkup, L. Janes, K. Woodward and F. Hovenden (eds) *The Gendered Cyborg: A Reader*, London: Routledge [previously published in *Communication* 10: 331 – 44].
Tracks science fiction's cyborgs, with a close eye on their genderings.

Bartsch, I., DiPalma, C. and Sells, L. (2001) 'Witnessing the postmodern jeremiad: (mis)understanding Donna Haraway's method of inquiry', *Configurations* 9: 127 – 64.
Compares the cyborg with the vampire figured in *Modest_Witness*, and discusses Florida's wetlands as vampiric and / or cyborgian landscape.
Campbell, K. (2004) 'The promise of feminist reflexivities: developing Donna Haraway's project for feminist science studies', *Hypatia* 19(1): 162 – 82.
Critical summary of Haraway's 'situated knowledged' work in the context of social studies of science and feminist studies of science.

Christie, J. (1992) 'A tragedy for cyborgs', *Configurations* 1: 171 – 96.
Discusses a number of intertextual cyborg connections across science fiction, postmodern writing, etc.

Clough, P. and Schneider, J. (2001) 'Donna J. Haraway', in A. Elliott and B. Turner (eds) *Profiles in Contemporary Social Theory*, London: Sage.
Decent, short summary of Haraway's life and work, tracking its influences and the ways it has itself influenced social theory broadly conceived.

Crewe, J. (1997) 'Transcoding the world: Haraway's postmodernism', *Signs* 22(4): 891 – 905
Reads Haraway's work as 'non-conforming' postmodernism, connecting it to branches of postmodern writing.

Currier, D. (2003) 'Feminist technological futures: Deleuze and body / technology assemblages', *Feminist Theory* 4(3): 321 – 38.
Critiques the take-up of the Cyborg Manifesto, and offers an alternative reading of body – technology connections based on philosophers Gilles Deleuze's and Felix Guattari's notion of the 'assemblage'.

Graham, E. (1999) 'Cyborgs or goddesses? Becoming divine in a cyberfeminist age', *Information, Communication & Society* 2(4): 419 – 38.
Springs from the Cyborg Manifesto's famous last line to consider a binary argued to have been left untroubled by Haraway: that between the divine and the secular. See also Graham 2002, in Other Work Cited.

Gray, C., Figueroa-Sarriera, H. and Mentor, S. (eds) (1995) *The Cyborg Handbook*, New York: Routledge.
Huge compendium of cyborg texts, shot through with Haraway's 'cyberquake'.

Kirkup, G., Janes, L., Woodward, K. and Hovenden F. (eds) (2000) *The Gendered Cyborg: a Reader*, London: Routledge.
A collection of key readings tracing the mutations of the Harawayan cyborg.

Munnik, R. (2001) 'Donna Haraway: cyborgs for earthly survival?', in H. Achterhuis (ed.) *American Philosophy of Technology: The Empirical Turn*, Bloomington IN: Indiana University Press.
A critical discussion of Haraway's life and work, mainly focused on the Cyborg Manifesto, and asking how radical cyborgs are.

Myerson, G. (2000) *Donna Haraway and GM Foods*, Cambridge: Icon.
Excellent little book introducing *Modest_Witness* through the lens of debates about genetically-modified foods.

Sandoval, C. (1995) 'New sciences: cyborg feminism and the methodology of the oppressed', in C. Gray, H. Figueroa-Sarriera and S. Mentor (eds) *The Cyborg Handbook*, New York: Routledge.
Both influenced by and influencing Haraway, Sandoval uses the idea of oppositional or differential consciousness to make a connection between 'US third world feminism' and cyborg feminism.

Schneider, J. (2005) *Donna Haraway: Live Theory*, London: Continuum.
Great general introduction, including an interview that summarizes many of Haraway's key ideas and concerns.

Scott, A. (2001) 'Trafficking in monstrosity: conceptualizations of "nature" within feminist cyborg discourses', *Feminist Theory* 2(3): 367 – 79.
Review essay making connections across and critiques of eight texts addressing 'cyborg discourses', including *Modest_Witness*. Useful for drawing a bigger picture of the 'cyberquake'.

Sofoulis, Z. (2002) 'Cyberquake: Haraway's manifesto', in D. Tofts, A. Jonson and A. Cavallaro (eds) *Prefiguring Cyberculture: An Intellectual History*, Cambridge MA: MIT Press.
Very useful discussion of the enduring impact of the Cyborg Manifesto, linking it to its generations of progeny, and tracing connections across bodies of work.

WORKS ABOUT CYBERCULTURE

Alaimo, S. (1994) 'Cyborg and ecofeminist interventions: challenges for environmental feminism', *Feminist Studies* 20: 133 – 52.

Bakardjieva, M. (2003) 'Virtual togetherness: an everyday life perspective', *Media, Culture & Society* 25: 291 – 313.

Balsamo, A. (1996) *Technologies of the Gendered Body: Reading Cyborg Women*, Durham NC: Duke University Press.

Bakardjieva, M. (2005) *Internet Society: The Internet in Everyday Life*, London: Sage.

Bakardjieva, M. and Smith, R. (2001) 'The internet in everyday life: computer networking from the standpoint of the domestic user', *New Media & Society* 3: 67 – 83.

Bell, D. (2001) *An Introduction to Cyberculture*, London: Routledge.

Bell, D., Loader, B., Pleace, N. and Schuler, D. (2004) *Cyberculture: the Key Concepts*, London: Routledge.

Benedikt, M. (ed.) (1991a) *Cyberspace: First Steps*, Cambridge MA: MIT Press.

Benedikt, M. (1991b) 'Cyberspace: some proposals', in M. Benedikt (ed.) *Cyberspace: First Steps*, Cambridge MA: MIT Press.

Benedikt, M. (1991c) 'Introduction', in M. Benedikt (ed.) *Cyberspace: First Steps*, Cambridge MA: MIT Press.

Dery, M. (1992) 'Cyberculture', *South Atlantic Quarterly* 91: 508 – 31.

Dery, M. (ed.) (1994) *Flame Wars: The Discourse of Cyberculture*, Durham NC: Duke University Press.

Gibson, W. (1984) *Neuromancer*, London: Grafton.

Gibson, W. (1991) 'Academy leader', in M. Benedikt (ed.) *Cyberspace: First Steps*, Cambridge MA: MIT Press.

Hine, C. (2000) *Virtual Ethnography*, London: Sage.

Lally, E. (2002) *At Home with Computers*, Oxford: Berg.

Lievrouw, L. (2004) 'What's changed about new media?', *New Media & Society* 6: 9 – 15.

Lykke, N. (1996) 'Between monsters, goddesses and cyborgs: feminist confrontations with science', in N.Lykke and R. Braidotti (eds) *Between Monsters, Goddesses and Cyborgs: Feminist Confrontations with Science, Medicine and Cyberspace*, London: Zed Books, pp. 13 – 29.

McCaffery, L. (ed.) (1991) *Storming the Reality Studio: A Casebook of Cyberpunk and Postmodern Science Fiction*, Durham NC: Duke University Press.

McCorduck, P. (1996) 'Sex, lies and avatars', *Wired* 4, available at http://www.wired.com/wired/archive/4.04/turkle_pr.html (accessed 19 October 2005).

Marshall, P. (2004) *New Media Cultures*, London: Arnold.

Miller, D. and Slater. D. (2000) *The Internet: An Ethnographic Approach*, Oxford: Berg.

Plant, S. (1995) 'The future looms: weaving women and cyberculture', *Body & Society* 1: 45 – 64.

Silver, D. (2000) 'Looking backwards, looking forwards: cyberculture studies 1990 – 2000', in D. Gauntlett (ed.) *Web.Studies*, London: Arnold.

Silver, D. (2004) 'Internet / cyberculture / digital culture / new media / fill-in-the-blanks studies', *New Media & Society* 6: 55 – 64.

Slouka, M. (1995) *War of the Worlds: The Assault on Reality*, New York: Basic Books.

Sobchack, V. (2000) 'New age mutant ninja hackers: reading *Mondo 2000*', in D. Bell and B. Kennedy (eds) *The Cybercultures Reader*, London: Routledge.

Stabile, C. (1994) *Feminism and the Technological Fix*, Manchester: Manchester University Press.

Sterne, J. (1999) 'Thinking the Internet: cultural studies versus the millennium', in S. Jones (ed.) *Doing Internet Research: Critical Issues and Methods for Examining the Net*, London: Sage.

Stoll, C. (1995) *Silicon Snake Oil: Second Thoughts on the Information Highway*, London: Pan.

Stone, A. R. (1995) *The War of Desire and Technology at the Close of the Mechanical Age*, Cambridge MA: MIT Press.

Szeto, G. (2002) 'Towards a general theory of value: an interview with Michael Benedikt', *Gain* 2.0, http://gain.aiga.org/content (accessed 19 October 2005).

Taylor, P. (2001) 'Informational intimacy and futuristic flu: love and confusion in the matrix', *Information, Communication and Society* 4: 74 – 94.

Thieme, R. (2000) 'Stalking the UFO meme', in D. Bell and B. Kennedy (eds) *The Cybercultures Reader*, London: Routledge.

Turkle, S. (1984) *The Second Self: Computers and the Human Spirit*, New York: Simon & Schuster.

Turkle, S. (1995) *Life on the Screen: Identity in the Age of the Internet*, London: Secker & Warburg.

Turkle, S. (1996) 'Who am we?' *Wired* 4, available from http://wired.com/wired/archive/4.01/turkle_pr.html (accessed 19 October 2005).

Turkle, S. (1998) 'Cyborg babies and cy-dough-plasm: ideas about self and life in the culture of simulation', in R. David-Floyd and J. Dumit (eds) *Cyborg Babies: From Techno-sex to Techno-tots*, New York: Routledge.

Turkle, S. (1999) 'What are we thinking about when we are thinking about computers?', in M. Biagioli (ed.) *The Science Studies Reader*, New York: Routledge.

Woodward, K. (1994) 'From virtual cyborgs to biological time bombs: technocriticism and the material body', in G. Bender and T. Druckrey (eds) *Culture on the Brink*, Seattle: Bay Press, pp. 47 – 64.

OTHER WORKS CITED

Those references not included in the previous sections, but cited in the book, are listed here.

Abbate, J. (2000) *Inventing the Internet*, Cambridge MA: MIT Press.

Amin, A. and Thrift, N. (2002) *Cities: Reimagining the Urban*, Cambridge: Polity.

Anderson, H. (2005) 'The tomorrow people', *Observer Technology Magazine* 1: 46 – 9.

Appadurai, A. (1990) 'Difference and disjuncture in the global cultural economy', in M. Featherstone (ed.) *Global Culture*, London: Sage.

Bell, D. (2005) *Science, Technology and Culture*, Maidenhead: Open University Press.

Braidotti, R. (1994) *Nomadic Subjects: Embodiment and Sexual Difference in Contemporary Feminist Theory*, New York: Columbia University Press.

Certeau, M. de (1984) *The Practice of Everyday Life*, Berkeley CA: University of California Press.

Clynes, M. and Kline, N. (1995 [1960]) 'Cyborgs and space', in C. Gray,

H. Figueroa-Sarriera and S. Mentor (eds) *The Cyborg Handbook*, New York: Routledge [originally published in *Astronautics*, September 1960].

Dant, T. (2005) *Materiality and Society*, Maidenhead: Open University Press.

Davis-Floyd, R. and Dumit, J. (eds) (1998) *Cyborg Babies: From Techno-sex to Techno-tots*, New York: Routledge.

Edgar, A. and Sedgwick, P. (1999) *Key Concepts in Cultural Theory*, London: Routledge.

Erikson, T. (2001) *The Tyranny of the Moment: Fast and Slow in the Information Age*, London: Pluto.

Florida, R. (2002) *The Rise of the Creative Class and How It's Transforming Work, Leisure, Community, and Everyday Life*, New York: Basic Books.

Flynn, B. (2003) 'Geography of the digital hearth', *Information, Communication and Society* 6: 551 – 76.

Frow, J. and Morris, M. (2000) 'Cultural studies', in N. Denzin and Y. Lincoln (eds) *The Handbook of Qualitative Research*, London: Sage.

Fuller, M. (2003) *Behind the Blip: Essays on the Culture of Software*, New York: Autonomedia.

Giddens, A. (1991) *The Transformation of Intimacy: Sexuality, Love and Eroticism in Modern Societies*, Cambridge: Polity.

Gonzalez, J. (2000 [1995]) 'Envisioning cyborg bodies: notes from current research', in G. Kirkup, L. Janes, K. Woodward and F. Hovenden (eds) *The Gendered Cyborg: A Reader*, London: Routledge [originally published in C. Gray, H. Figueroa-Sarriera and S. Mentor (eds) *The Cyborg Handbook*, New York: Routledge].

Graham, E. (2002) *Representations of the Post / human: Monsters, Aliens and Others in Popular Culture*, Manchester, Manchester University Press.

Graham, S. (ed.) (2003) *The Cybercities Reader*, London: Routledge.

Graham, S. and Marvin, S. (2001) *Splintering Urbanism: Networked Infrastructures, Technological Mobilities and the Urban Condition*, London: Routledge.

Gray, C. (2001) *Cyborg Citizen: Politics in the Posthuman Stage*, New York: Routledge.

Gunkel, D. (2005) 'Editorial: introduction to hacking and hacktivism', *New Media & Society* 7: 595 – 7.

Halberstam, J. (1991) 'Automating gender: postmodern feminism in the age of the intelligent machine', *Feminist Studies* 7(3): 439 – 60.

Hall, S. (1973) *Encoding and Decoding in the Television Discourse*, Birmingham: CCCS Stencilled Paper 7.

Harvey, D. (1989) *The Condition of Postmodernity: An Enquiry into the Origins of Cultural Change*, Oxford: Blackwell.

Hetherington, K. (1998) *Expressions of Identity: Space, Performance, Politics*, London: Sage.

Highmore, B. (2002) *Everyday Life and Cultural Theory*, London: Routledge.

Himanen, P. (2001) *The Hacker Ethic and the Spirit of the Information Age*, London: Secker & Warburg.

Ihde, D. (1990) *Technology and the Lifeworld: From Garden to Earth*, Bloomington IN: Indiana University Press.

Jary, D. and Jary, J. (2000) *Collins Dictionary of Sociology*, Glasgow: HarperCollins.

Jayne, M. (2005) *Cities and Consumption*, London: Routledge.

Kirby, V. (1997) *Telling Flesh: The Substance of the Corporeal*, London: Routledge.

Lane, R. (2000) *Jean Baudrillard*, London: Routledge.

Latour, B. (1993) *We Have Never Been Modern*, Hemel Hemstead: Harvester Wheatsheaf.

Lefebvre, H. (1971) *Everyday Life in the Modern World*, London: Harper & Row.

Lefebvre, H. (1991) *Critique of Everyday Life,Volume 1*, London: Verso.

Lehtonen, T.-K. (2003) 'The domestication of new technologies as a set of trials', *Journal of Consumer Culture* 3: 363 – 85.

Lykke, N. and Braidotti, R. (eds) (1996) *Between Monsters, Goddesses and Cyborgs: Feminist Confrontations with Science, Medicine and Cyberspace*, London: Zed Books.

Margolis, J. (2000) *A Brief History of Tomorrow: The Future, Past and Present*, London: Bloomsbury.

Michael, M. (2000) *Reconnecting Culture, Technology and Nature: From Society to Heterogeneity*, London: Routledge.

Moseley, R. (2000) 'Makeover takeover on British television', *Screen* 41: 299 – 314.

O'Sullivan, T. (2005) 'From television lifestyle to lifestyle television', in D. Bell and J. Hollows (eds) *Ordinary Lifestyles: Popular Media, Consumption and Taste*, Buckingham: Open University Press.

Oehlert, M. (1995) 'From Captain America to Wolverine: cyborgs in comic books, alternative images of cybernetic heroes and villains', in C. Gray, H. Figueroa-Sarriera and S. Mentor (eds) *The Cyborg Handbook*, New York: Routledge.

Parkins, W. and Craig, G. (2006) *Slow Living*, Oxford: Berg.

Rheingold, H. (1991) *Virtual Reality*, New York: Summit.

Ross, A. (2000) 'Hacking away at the counterculture', in D. Bell and B. Kennedy (eds) *The Cybercultures Reader*, London: Routledge.

Ross, A. (2003) *No-collar: The Humane Workplace and its Hidden Costs*, New York: Basic Books.

Sassen, S. (1999) 'Digital networks and power', in M. Featherstone and S. Lash (eds) *Spaces of Culture*, London: Sage.

Scannell, P. (1996) *Radio, Television and Modern Life*, Oxford: Blackwell.

Shields, R. (2002) *The Virtual*, London: Routledge.

Spigel, L. (1992) *Make Room for TV: Television and the Family Ideal in Postwar America*, Chicago IL: University of Chicago Press.

Stallabrass, J. (1999) 'The ideal city and the virtual hive: modernism and emergent order in computer culture', in J. Downey and J. McGuigan (eds) *Technocities: The Culture and Political Economy of the Digital Revolution*, London: Sage.

Stone, A. R. (1991) 'Will the real body please stand up? Boundary stories about virtual cultures', in M. Benedikt (ed.) *Cyberspace: First Steps*, Cambridge MA: MIT Press.

Tofts, D., Jonson, A. and Cavallaro, A. (eds) (2002) *Prefiguring Cyberculture: An Intellectual History*, Cambridge MA: MIT Press.

Tomas, D. (1991) 'Old rituals for new space: *rites de passage* and William Gibson's cultural model of cyberspace', in M. Benedikt (ed.) *Cyberspace: First Steps*, Cambridge MA: MIT Press.

Tomas, D. (2000) 'The technophilic body: on technicity in William Gibson's cyborg culture', in D. Bell and B. Kennedy (eds) *The Cybercultures Reader*, London: Routledge.

Van Dijk, J. (2005) 'From shoebox to performative agent: the computer as personal memory machine', *New Media & Society* 7(3): 311 – 32.

Weedon, C. (1999) *Feminism, Theory and the Politics of Difference*, Oxford: Blackwell.

Williams, R. (1974) *Television: Technology and Cultural Form*, London: Fontana.

Williams, R. (1976) *Keywords: A Vocabulary of Culture and Society*, London: Fontana.

Zylinska, J. (ed.) (2002) *The Cyborg Experiments: The Extensions of the Body in the Media Age*, London: Continuum.

INDEX

Bold numbers denote main treatments.
Italic page numbers denote boxed text.

viruses *33*
visibility 22, 25–27
VR (virtual reality) *19*, 82–83; real
    virtuality 77–87

War of the Worlds 10
Weber, M. 55
weblogs 78
Webster, Frank 60, 90
Wiener, Norbert *3*

Williams, Raymond 5, 40
Wired (magazine) 10–11, 91
women of color 102, 106
Woodward, Kathleen 112
work ethic 66
work, feminization of 104
World 3–18, *18*, 50
world economy 61

xenotransplantation 101

Printed and bound by CPI Group (UK) Ltd, Croydon, CR0 4YY

01/11/2024

01782627-0001